THE GREAT WALT DISNEY WORLD SCAVENGER HUNT

A DETAILED PATH THROUGH
MAGIC KINGDOM, EPCOT,
DISNEY'S ANIMAL KINGDOM AND
DISNEY'S HOLLYWOOD STUDIOS

CATHERINE F. OLEN

The Great Walt Disney World Scavenger Hunt
A Detailed Path through the Magic Kingdom, Epcot, Disney's Animal Kingdom and Disney's Hollywood Studios
© 2020 Catherine Olen

All Rights Reserved. No Portion of this book may be reproduced, stored in a retrieval system, or transmitted in any form or by any means – electronic, mechanical, photocopy, recording, scanning or other – except for brief quotations in critical reviews or articles, without the prior written permission of the publisher. Subject to permission under section 107 and/or 108 of the 1976 United States Copyright act. Requests for permission should be addressed to the publisher wwww.mousehangover.com. 949-234-7332
First paperback edition February 2020
ISBN 978-1-64822-000-5 (paperback)
ISBN 978-1-64822-001-2 (eBook)

Published by Mouse Hangover
www.Mousehangover.com

Please note: Every effort has been made to ensure the accuracy of information throughout this book. The information is believed to be accurate at the time of printing. The publish and author are not responsible for errors or omissions, for changes to details or the consequences of the readers reliance to the information provided.

Attraction closures or updates are not the responsibility of the publisher or author and can not be guaranteed at the time of use of this book.

Readers are welcome to contact the publisher for comments, updates or questions.

About the Author

Catherine Olen has been visiting Disney parks since she was a small child. Olen fell in love with the parks built through the imagination of Walt Disney and became an annual passholder in 1991 and has held an annual pass ever since.

Olen first traveled to Walt Disney World at the age of thirty, immediately falling in love with the Florida parks. She has traveled to the Walt Disney World theme parks each year since and now travels to Orlando several times a year to revel in the new attractions as well as the classic favorites.

Olen now shares her love of all things Disney in *The Great Walt Disney World Scavenger Hunt*.

Come Check Us Out

Check out new books, video and news at
www.Mousehangover.com
Subscribe to Mouse Hangover
Instagram - @TheMouseHangover
Twitter - @Mousehangover
Facebook - @Mousehangover
@WDWScavengerHunt

Youtube – Mouse Hangover

Other books:

The Great Disneyland Scavenger Hunt
The Great Universal Studios Hollywood Scavenger Hunt
The Great Universal Orlando Scavenger Hunt

Dedication

To Lynne Dunn for being my twin in love of everything Disney

To everyone who gave me their support and assistance in the process of finishing this book

To Every person that has fallen in love with Walt Disney World resort

Lastly, my thanks to Walt Disney for the vision that created Disneyland and all of the cast members who have made this adventure a magical experience.

Table of Contents

Introduction xiii

Magic Kingdom 1
Esplanade 2
Main Street U.S.A. 3
- Walt Disney World Railroad Main Street 3
- Main Street Firehouse 5
- Harmony Barber Shop 6
- Emporium 7
- Main Street Confectionary 8
- Casey's Corner 9

HUB 11
Fantasyland 12
- Cinderella Castle 12
- Sir Mickey's 13
- Castle Couture 14
- The Many Adventures of Winnie the Pooh 15
- Mickey's PhilharMagic 17
- Seven Dwarfs Mine Train 19
- Mad Tea Party 20
- Storybook Circus 20
- Pete's Silly Sideshow 21
- Casey Jr. Splash 'N' Soak Station 22
- The Barnstormer 22
- Dumbo the Flying Elephant 23
- Be Our Guest Restaurant 23
- Enchanted Tales with Belle 25

    Gaston's Tavern 26
    Under the Sea – Journey of the Little Mermaid 26
    Pinocchio Village Haus 28
    Peter Pan's Flight 29
    It's a Small World 31
    Tangled area 33
Liberty Square 35
    Liberty Square Riverboat 35
    The Hall of Presidents 37
    The Haunted Mansion 40
Adventureland 45
    Swiss Family Robinson Treehouse 45
    Walt Disney's Enchanted Tiki Room 47
    Jungle Cruise 48
    Pirates of the Caribbean 52
Frontierland 54
    Country Bear Jamboree 54
    Frontierland Shooting Gallery 55
    Splash Mountain 56
    Briar Patch 58
    Walt Disney Railroad Frontierland Station 59
    Big Thunder Mountain Railroad 60
    Tom Sawyer Island 63
Tomorrowland 65
    Buzz Lightyear's Space Ranger Spin 65
    Walt Disney's Carousel of Progress 67
    Monster's Inc. Laugh Floor 70
    Tomorrowland Transit Authority PeopleMover 71

EPCOT 75
Introduction 76
    Future World East 77
    Spaceship Earth 77
    Mission SPACE 80

Test Track	82
Future World West	84
The Land	84
Living with the Land	85
Soarin' Around the World	86
The Seas with Nemo and Friends	89
The Seas with Nemo and Friends attraction	89
SeaBase	91
Imagination!	93
Journey into Imagination with Figment	93
World Showcase	96
Canada	96
O' Canada	97
United Kingdom	99
France	100
Morocco	101
Japan	102
The American Adventure	103
The American Adventure	104
Italy	108
Germany	108
China	109
Reflections of China	109
Norway	111
Frozen Ever After	111
Mexico	113
Grand Fiesta Tour starring the Three Caballeros	114
Disney Hollywood Studios	117
Introduction	118
Hollywood Blvd	119
Oscar's Super Service	119
Celebrity 5 & 10	122
Adrian and Edith's	123

- The Brown Derby 124
- Sunset Blvd 126
  - Rockin' Roller Coaster Starring Aerosmith 127
  - Twilight Zone Tower of Terror 128
  - Carthay Circle 131
- Echo Lake 133
  - 50's Prime Time Cafe 133
  - Indiana Jones Epic Stunt Spectacular! 136
  - Star Tours – The Adventure Continues 137
- Grand Avenue 140
  - Muppet Vision 3D 140
  - Stage 1 Company Store 146
  - Mama Melrose Ristorante Italiano 149
  - PizzeRizzo 151
- Star Wars: Galaxy's Edge 153
  - Oga's Cantina 155
  - Millennium Falcon: Smugglers Run 155
  - Dok-Ondar's Den of Antiquities 157
  - Star Wars: Rise of the Resistance 159
- Toy Story Land 162
  - Toy Story Mania! 163
  - Alien Swirling Saucers 169
  - Woody's Lunch Box 170
  - Slinky Dog Dash 172
- Animation Courtyard 175
  - Walt Disney Presents – Gallery and Exhibits 175
  - Walt Disney: One Man's Dream 179
  - The Voyage of the Little Mermaid 181

Disney's Animal Kingdom 183
- Introduction 184
- Discovery Island 185
  - It's Tough to be a Bug 186

- Africa 191
  - Kilimanjaro Safaris 192
  - Gorilla Falls Exploration Trail 195
- Pandora – The World of Avatar 197
  - Na'Vi River Journey 199
  - Avatar Flight of Passage 199
- Asia 206
  - Maharaja Jungle Trek 207
  - Expedition Everest – Legend of the
    Forbidden Mountain 209
- Dinoland U.S.A. 212
  - The Boneyard 213
  - Primeval Whirl 215
  - Chester and Hester's Dinosaur Treasures 216
  - DINOSAUR 218
  - Dino-Bytes Snacks 221
  - Restaurantosaurus 221

Answer Key 225

Introduction

The great vision of Walt Disney allowed for the magnificence that is the Walt Disney World resort. Calling this theme park a "World" is correct. While Walt Disney did not live to see his dream realized, the Walt Disney World resort stands as a monument to this great man and his vision.

My first pilgrimage to Walt Disney world would not be until my mid-thirties. Not realizing how different the Walt Disney World resort was from the Disneyland resort, I naively asked a cast member if I could walk from the Magic Kingdom to Epcot. She barely held a laugh while informing me there was significant distance between the various theme park areas. It took only a short time before I was navigating the parks, from Magic Kingdom to Animal Kingdom with ease, just like the seasoned guests I saw all around me. Over the years, my trips to Orlando have been more frequent and my love for Walt Disney World grows each time I step through the gates of this magical place.

Some of my fondest memories have been cultivated since my first trip to Walt Disney World. Being grand marshal in the parade and riding in Walt Disney's personal car, being married by Winnie the Pooh, with Piglet and Tigger in the wedding party in the UK pavilion and my daughters first trip to the theme parks. All these memories are truly treasured by me and our family.

While Walt Disney never had the opportunity to see these parks for himself, the imagineers have done his memory proud. I can only imagine what Walt's speech would have been on the opening day of the Magic Kingdom, but his brother Roy made him proud on that day, October 1, 1971.

Many people have asked me what my favorite attraction is or which of the theme parks is my favorite. There is no definitive answer to this question as my list is different depending on what age and experiences I have had throughout my life. While Disneyland will always be my home, Walt Disney World holds memories each time I revisit The Country Bear Jamboree, ride with the animals of Africa, travel through the Hollywood Tower Hotel or travel the countries of the World Showcase.

I invite you to use the pages within this book to see the Walt Disney World theme parks through new eyes. Whether this is your first visit or five hundredth, I challenge you to finish this book and *not* find something new to enjoy within the borders of the Walt Disney World resort.

This book is dedicated to the vision of Walt Disney.

While Walt Disney World will never be complete, Walt Disney's spirit and dream remain a constant part of the charm Walt Disney World holds in the hearts of all who enter her gates.

The Great Walt Disney World Scavenger Hunt

How to use this book:

Your Disney trivia is broken down into three categories

- One star – Easier questions – Good for families with small children or first-time guests
- Two stars – Challenging questions – For returning guests and those with more time
- Three stars – Expert questions – For those looking for a real challenge or Disney park experts

All of the questions found in this book have been verified by several Disney enthusiasts and I am aware that the décor of Walt Disney World changes regularly. If there are changes, you can visit www.MouseHangover.com for current updates. If you have come across a change prior to finding the update on my website, please email me so the changes can be noted.

I hope you find your way through the Walt Disney World resort with new eyes and enjoy your hunt for the loving details Walt Disney wanted his guests to experience.

Note: All content is subject to change without notice. Ride closures, construction, or overlays for the Halloween and Christmas holidays may alter the content temporarily due to park-wide decorations.

Trademarks:

This book contains Disney copy-righted characters, registered trademarks, marks, and registered marks of The Walt Disney Company and Disney Enterprises Inc.

All references to these properties, and The Twilight Zone®, a registered trademark of CBS, Inc., are made solely for editorial purposes. Neither the author nor the publisher makes any commercial claim to their use, and neither is affiliated with The Walt Disney Company or CBS in any way.

All references to the properties of Aerosmith, Indiana Jones, Avatar, Star Wars and any second party characters of films are made solely for editorial purposes. Neither the author nor the publisher makes any commercial claims to their use and neither is affiliated to these works or the producing entities.

Magic Kingdom

As you enter this magical place, take a moment to let yourself be transported to a land of enchantment. Fly on a magic carpet or sing with the birds in Adventureland. Join your favorite animated characters as you ride with The Little Mermaid or Peter Pan. Allow yourself to be taken to the future with Space Mountain or laugh yourself silly with the gang from Monstropolis.

Finally, join your favorite princesses in front of Cinderella castle for a celebration in fireworks to create memories for years to come.

Join *the Great Walt Disney World Scavenger Hunt* as we take you on a tour of discovery to help you fall in love with this magical place.

Esplanade

Even before you walk through the gates of the Magic Kingdom, the enchantment begins in the esplanade. Stop for a moment to look around you at the sights and smells of Magic Kingdom as the anticipation mounts of the wonders to behold within the gates.

1. ✯ As you read the window of The Magic Kingdom railroad, what is the middle initial of Walter Disney?
   a. O
   b. E
   c. W
   d. D

2. ✯✯ As you enter the tunnel to Main Street on either the right or left side, what is the tenth word of the dedication on the bronze plaque above your head?
   a. Yesterday
   b. Fantasy
   c. World
   d. Tomorrow

Did you know?

Walt Disney World falls in three different postal codes 32836, 32821 and 34787. You can mail your post cards from Walt Disney World resort by dropping them into any of the mail-boxes throughout the theme parks.

Main Street U.S.A.

Main Street U.S.A. was fashioned after Walt Disney's beloved Marceline, Missouri at the turn of the century. Take a stroll back in time as you discover the wonders within this quaint street.

Walt Disney World Railroad Main Street

1. ★★ As you look around the Main Street train station find the painting entitled *Spanning the Continent*. What made the railroads possible according to the bronze plaque?
    a. America's Men
    b. America's Forests
    c. America's Railroads
    d. America's Steel

2. ★★ Find the painting entitled *A Golden Spike is Driven*. Which U.S. President made a statement via telegraph about this great accomplishment?
    a. Ulysses Grant
    b. Abraham Lincoln
    c. William Taft
    d. Ronald Reagan

> ### Did you know?
> Within Main Street train station, you will find a turn of the century football game. This game is a wonderful example of the precursor to the video game arcades we saw in the 1980's.

3. ★ As you stand before the Walt Disney World Music Box Collection in the train station, which of these is *not* one of the instruments listed?
   - a. Piano
   - b. Drum
   - c. Triangle
   - d. Castanets

4. ★★ Walk up to the ticket window outside the station on the second level. What item sits on the empty seat?
   - a. Engineers cap
   - b. Hard hat
   - c. Lantern
   - d. Gloves

5. ★★★ On the back wall of the ticket booth you will find a red box. According to the sign, what does this box call?
   - a. Messenger
   - b. Conductor
   - c. Engineer
   - d. Police

6. ★★★ On the desk, you will find a binder with several papers in it. According to the Harper's Weekly, it is the journal of what?
   - a. Medicine
   - b. Railroad
   - c. Civilization
   - d. Train tracks

7. ★★★ Within the ticket window office, you will find a notice with the outline for Children's fares. What is the minimum fare for children of the half fare age?
   - a. Five cents
   - b. Twenty-five cents
   - c. Twelve cents
   - d. Ten cents

8. ★ As you walk down the steps and to the tunnel beneath the Main Street Station, you will find a shadow box with die cast trains within, what is the name of the train on the bottom row in the center?
    a. Mallard
    b. Royal Hudson
    c. Big Boy
    d. Adler

9. ★★★ As you look around the tunnel, you will find a shadow box with buttons displayed within. What is the year of the 14th annual reunion of the A & C.W. employees?
    a. 1808
    b. 1708
    c. 2008
    d. 1908

10. ★★ Find the shadow box with a pass for Mrs. N.J. Jacobs from Northern Pacific Railroad within. Mrs. Jacobs is the wife of which railroad staff?
    a. Engineman
    b. Conductor
    c. Engineer
    d. Porter

11. ★ As you stand before the Chamber of Commerce on Main Street USA, in what year was it established?
    a. 1955
    b. 1971
    c. 1855
    d. 1871

Main Street Firehouse

12. ★ As you stand before the Main Street firehouse, what is the engine company number?
    a. 71
    b. 55
    c. 17
    d. 19

13. ★★ Within the firehouse, you will find the Equitable Powder mfg. co box lid. What does this company manufacture?
    a. Flea Powder
    b. Talcum Powder
    c. Blasting Powder
    d. Foot Powder

14. ★★★ Within the Main Street Firehouse, you will find the Fireman's Prayer. As you read this prayer, finish this line, "And hear the weakest _____."
    a. Voice
    b. Shout
    c. Person
    d. Cry

15. ★★ As you exit the fire station you will find the car barn, within you will find two barrels, what is contained in the larger barrel?
    a. Car parts
    b. Rain water
    c. Rubber hoses
    d. Horseshoe nails

Harmony Barber Shop

> **Did you know?**
>
> You can get your haircut at the Magic Kingdom. Make a reservation before your next trip to the Walt Disney World resort. The baby's first haircut includes a certificate and a pair of mouse ears for your little one.

16. ★★ On the corner, you will find Harmony Barber Shop. As you enter the shop, how much is baby's first haircut?
    a. $18.00
    b. $25.00
    c. $7.00
    d. $19.00

17. ★★ Next door to Harmony Barber shop is the Emporium, as you look at the windows above, you will find the Rainbow Paint Co. Which of these is not one of the colors in the rainbow?

a.	Blue	c.	Yellow
b.	Purple	d.	Green

Emporium

18. ★★★ As you come to the corner you will find the Emporium sign above the doorway to the store. How many light bulbs surround the outside of this sign?
    a. 56
    b. 76
    c. 66
    d. 46

19. ★★ As you look in the windows of the Emporium, you will find scenes from your favorite Disney animated films. According to the brass plaque beneath Snow White, who did the Evil Queen disguise herself as to poison the princess?
    a. A witch
    b. A Dwarf
    c. An apple seller
    d. A peddler

20. ★★ Find the window for The Little Mermaid outside of the Emporium. What is Ursula's evil plot according to the brass plaque?
    a. Capture Ariel
    b. Take over the undersea kingdom
    c. Capture King Triton
    d. Marry Prince Eric

21. ★★ According to the brass plaque for Beauty and the Beast, what year did this film come out in theaters?
    a. 1989
    b. 1990
    c. 1991
    d. 1992

Bonus question:

22. ★★★ As you look in the window with the ballroom scene from Beauty and the Beast, you will find several

characters look on at the dancing couple. Which of these characters is *not* present?

   a. Feather duster   c. Wardrobe
   b. Foot stool   d. Mrs. Potts

23. ✯✯ If you cross the street and approach the flag pole, you will find a bronze plaque with the opening day speech of Walt Disney World. What is the forty-fourth word in this speech?

   a. Inspiration   c. Joy
   b. Knowledge   d. Disney

Did you know?

On the opposite side of Main Street, you will find a restaurant with the name Tony's. This is reference to Tony's from the Disney film *Lady and the Tramp* when Tramp and Lady share a plate of spaghetti. Look at the décor within and see the statue of Lady and Tramp as well as photos from this classic film.

Did you know?

If you look at the sidewalk outside of Tony's, you will find a heart carved into the cement with two set of paw prints. This lovely heart stands as a testament to Lady and Tramps love.

Main Street Confectionary

24. ✯ As you continue your way down Main Street you come to the Main Street Confectionary. Within the door, you

will find an advertisement for cotton candy, finish this line, "Soft as a _____."
   a. Cotton ball
   b. Baby's bottom
   c. Bunnies fur
   d. Cloud

25. ★★ As you explore the Confectionary, you will find a sign entitled Toasting. What city was the newfangled ironworks found in?
   a. New York
   b. Chicago
   c. Orlando
   d. Anaheim

26. ★★ Find the sign referring to the invention of breaking open the coco beans. Finish the title of this sign, "Breaking & _____."
   a. Entering
   b. Cracking
   c. Winnowing
   d. Cooking

---

27. ★★ Work your way down Main Street to the Crystal Arts shop. Within the store, you will find a workshop with kilns and equipment. What famous United States landmark appears on the calendar on the wall?
   a. Capitol Building
   b. Statue of Liberty
   c. Mount Rushmore
   d. Lincoln Memorial

Casey's Corner

28. ★★★ At the end of Main Street, you will find Casey's Corner. As you step inside, look around at the memorabilia on the walls. How much is the admission for the baseball game between New Hartford and Clinton H.S.?
   a. 15 cents
   b. 25 cents
   c. 5 cents
   d. 18 cents

29. ★★ As you look at the scoreboard, how many runs did Mudville score?
    a. 4 runs
    b. 6 runs
    c. 1 run
    d. 2 runs

30. ★★★ According to the newspaper for the Married vs Singles game. What is the name of the short stop on the married team?
    a. Butcher Boy Orton
    b. Chipmunk Brady
    c. Ace Wood
    d. Spike Clark

31. ★★★ As you continue reading this paper, what is furnished to persons not wanting to hear the calls between the players?
    a. Face masks
    b. Ear plugs
    c. Ear muffs
    d. Helmets

HUB

The hub of the Magic Kingdom is the entryway to the various lands. This area offers guests grass to relax on your travels with charming bronze statues of your favorite Disney characters throughout.

Cinderella castle stands high above welcoming guests to Fantasyland. Tomorrowland waits for those looking for adventure while the entrance to Adventureland is hidden from view. Liberty Square takes guests to the origins of our country and brings history to life.

1. ☆ At the center of the hub stands the Partners statue dedicated to Walt Disney. As you read the plaque on this statue, which of these is the tenth word in the quote?
   a. Children
   b. Family
   c. Parents
   d. Park

Did you know?

Throughout the day, you can see your favorite Disney characters sing and dance on the stage in front of Cinderella Castle. Be sure to spend some time with your Magic Kingdom friends.

Fantasyland

Cross over the draw bridge and relive your favorite animated Disney films when you step into Fantasyland. Become a prince or princess, ride on a runaway mine train, or fly above the rooftops of London. Within Fantasyland your fondest childhood dreams become reality when you fly on Dumbo and spin the teacups on your own mad tea party.

Cinderella Castle

1. ★★★ As you walk through Cinderella Castle, look at the mosaics depicting scenes from the film *Cinderella*. Which of these is *not* one of the scenes you see?
    a. Cinderella and Fairy Godmother
    b. Mice turn into horses
    c. Trying on the glass slipper
    d. Invitation to the ball

Did you know?

Within Cinderella castle there is a full-service restaurant called Cinderella's Royal Table. Make your reservation for this once in a lifetime experience. While dining, you may even meet your favorite Disney princesses.

2. ★★★ High above you within the castle is Cinderella's Royal Table, a fine dining experience for guests. Enter the foyer of the castle and look at the rafter high above you, what animated characters from the film do you see?
   a. Blue birds
   c. Gus and Jack
   b. Lucifer the cat
   d. Fairy godmother

3. ★★ Outside Cinderella castle you will find a wishing well. As you see the mice around the base of the well, what does Gus hold in his hands?
   a. A sash
   c. A book
   b. A coin
   d. Beads

Bonus Question:

4. ★★★ You will find Lady Tremaine's cat chasing the mice around the well. What is the name of this cat?
   a. Lucifer
   c. Thomas O'Malley
   b. Toulouze
   d. Phillipe

Sir Mickey's

5. ★★★ Across from Cinderella castle in Fantasyland you will find Sir Mickey's shop. What famous animated character do you find peaking in from the roof as you stand in this shop?
   a. Willie the giant
   c. Genie
   b. The Sorcerer
   d. Mickey Mouse

Did you know?

Above the left doorway of Sir Mickey's, you will find a framed picture of a valley with a castle in the distance. This is Happy Valley from the cartoon *Mickey and the Beanstalk* in which the golden harp is stolen by the giant.

> **Did you know?**
>
> Look to the right of this same doorway and you will find several spools of thread, a pair of scissors and a ruler. These items were left behind by Mickey Mouse from the cartoon *The Brave Little Tailor*.

Sir Mickey's is a compilation of these two cartoons, both costarring Willie the Giant as the foe of our hero Mickey Mouse.

Castle Couture

6. ★★ Across the street is Castle Couture, within this shop you will find the gown made for Sleeping Beauty waiting for the princess to dance the night away with her prince. In the stained glass, you will find the three good fairies, which of these is not one of the names of the fairies?
    a. Flora
    b. Fauna
    c. Merriweather
    d. Clairette

> **Did you know?**
>
> If you watch the Sleeping Beauty gown, you will see it turn from blue to pink and back. Listen carefully as you hear the voices of the fairies arguing about which color the gown should be.

> **Did you know?**
>
> As you look around Castle Couture, you will find the pink gown that was Cinderella's mothers' gown. Cinderella has left it in the middle of altering to do another of her chores.

The Great Walt Disney World Scavenger Hunt

> ### Did you know?
> As you look around the room, notice the circular photo frames with silhouettes within them. Each frame shows the silhouette of a different Disney princess.

> ### Did you know?
> Outside of Castle Couture shop is the Cinderella Fountain. If you look closely at the pink background you will notice a crown. If you crouch down at child level, the crown aligns with Cinderella's head to make a perfect crown for her statue.

The Many Adventures of Winnie the Pooh

7. ★ As you approach the queue for The Many Adventures of Winnie the Pooh, what name appears above the doorway to Pooh's house?
   a. Winnie the Pooh
   b. Christopher Robin
   c. A.A. Milne
   d. Mr. Sanders

8. ★ Take a close look at Winnie the Pooh's mailbox. What common item does he use for the mailbox flag?
   a. Flyswatter
   b. Spatula
   c. Spoon
   d. Shovel

9. ★★ As you enter the queue, look at the storybook pages across from you. What color is the balloon Christopher Robin holds out for Pooh?
   a. Red
   b. Blue
   c. Green
   d. Yellow

> **Did you know?**
>
> As you work your way through the queue for The Many Adventures of Winnie the Pooh, pause at the walls of honey. As you brush your hand across the dripping honey you will reveal Pooh's friends beneath the gooey honey.

10. ★★ As you enter your ride vehicle and begin your journey, read the first page you see. Which wind traded places with the west wind?
    a. North
    b. Arctic
    c. East
    d. South

11. ★ As you see Kanga and Roo in the blustery day, what color is the scarf little Roo hangs onto?
    a. Blue
    b. Yellow
    c. Green
    d. Red

> **Did you know?**
>
> If you look closely at a secret spot within Owl's house, you will find a photo a Mr. Toad handing Owl the deed to his property. This appears due to the fact that this was the original home to Mr. Toad's Wild Ride attraction.

12. ★★ As you enter Owl's house you will find dishes stacked on a shelf high above your head. How many plates are stacked beneath the tea cup?
    a. 3
    b. 4
    c. 5
    d. 1

The Great Walt Disney World Scavenger Hunt

13. ★ As you exit Owl's house which character greets you through a hole in the story page?
    a. Tigger
    b. Winnie the Pooh
    c. Owl
    d. Gofer

14. ★★ How many times do you see Tigger in the bouncing scene of the ride, including the time he jumps on Pooh?
    a. 4
    b. 3
    c. 7
    d. 5

15. ★ In the Heffalump and Woozles scene, what colors do you see on the yoyo?
    a. White and black
    b. Pink and blue
    c. Blue and green
    d. Red and white

16. ★ In the rain and flood scene, what does Piglet stand on to avoid getting wet?
    a. A Hunny pot
    b. An umbrella
    c. A chair
    d. A log

17. ★★ On your way to the end of the Many Adventures of Winnie the Pooh, you will encounter several storybook pages in front of you. Which word appears on the page diagonally unlike the rest?
    a. End
    b. Yawn
    c. Bounce
    d. Pooh

18. ★★ Which character asks Pooh, 'Wasn't that fun?" according to the storybook pages?
    a. Piglet
    b. Tigger
    c. Rabbit
    d. Christopher Robin

Mickey's PhilharMagic

19. ★★ As you stand beneath the large statue of Mickey Mouse above the queue for Mickey's PhilHarmagic, what does he hold in his hand?

a.	A baton	c.	A trombone
b.	Sheet music	d.	A sorcerer's hat

20. ★ As you enter the queue, how many tuba's do you see painted on the wall?
    a. 4
    b. 3
    c. 2
    d. 1

21. ★ As you walk through the line, read some of the posters featuring upcoming acts to the theater. Which of the character sings Torch songs according to the posters?
    a. Maleficent
    b. Captain Hook
    c. Donald Duck
    d. Hades

22. ★ As you continue your look at the posters, what does the Wheezy poster say about his show?
    a. Appearing in Fantasyland
    b. Final weeks
    c. Final squeaks
    d. Closing soon

Did you know?

If you listen carefully just before the theater doors open, you will hear the voice of stage manager Goofy directing you.

23. ★ As you take your seat and the curtain opens, what does Mickey Mouse find Donald Duck doing?
    a. Sleeping
    b. Playing instruments
    c. Eating
    d. Dusting the instruments

24. ★★ Which instruments gives Donald duck a hard time by continuing to play music after the rest of the instruments stop?
    a. Violin
    b. Flute
    c. Piano
    d. Drum

The Great Walt Disney World Scavenger Hunt

25. ★★★ Which of these is *not* one of the songs you heard during Mickey's PhilharMagic?
    a. "So This is Love"
    b. "Be Our Guest"
    c. "I Just Can't Wait to be King"
    d. "A Whole New World"

> ### Did you know?
> On the Prince Charming Regal Carousel attraction there is a special horse just like the carousel at Disneyland. Look for the horse with the gold ribbon tied to its tail. This special horse belongs to none other than Cinderella herself.

Seven Dwarfs Mine Train

26. ★ As you enter the queue for the Seven Dwarfs Mine Train, what color is the gem stone that appears on the sign?
    a. Blue
    b. White
    c. Green
    d. Red

27. ★★ As your ride begins and you enter the mine where the dwarves are working, which dwarf is sitting in the mine car with the jewels?
    a. Happy
    b. Dopey
    c. Grumpy
    d. Sneezy

28. ★ What kind of woodland creature sleeps with Sleepy in the mine?
    a. Rabbit
    b. Squirrel
    c. Deer
    d. Skunk

29. ★★ What is the time that appears on the clock you see within the mine?
    a. 4:00
    b. 3:00
    c. 5:00
    d. 6:00

> ### Did you know?
> As you come to the end of your ride, look at the dwarfs cottage to your right. You will see Snow White dancing with the dwarfs. This scene is taken directly from the original *Snow White and the Seven Dwarfs* film.

Mad Tea Party

30. ✯ As you read the sign in front of Mad Tea Party, what color is the teapot the dormouse is peeking out of?
    a. Blue
    b. Green
    c. Yellow
    d. Pink

> ### Did you know?
> As you watch the teapot in the center of the Mad Tea Party attraction, you will see the Dormouse peeking out at you every few seconds.

Storybook Circus

31. ✯ As you enter Storybook Circus, pause for a moment to read the banner advertising the wonders that await you. On the Casey Jr. Banner, what sort of animal is the engineer on the train?
    a. Giraffe
    b. Bear
    c. Lion
    d. Monkey

32. ✯ On the banner for the Barnstormer, finish the line, "Soarin' to _____ Heights.»
    a. Astonishing
    b. Ridiculous
    c. Stupendous
    d. Silly

The Great Walt Disney World Scavenger Hunt

Pete's Silly Sideshow

33. ★★ As you come to the entrance of the big top for Pete's Silly Sideshow, take a look at the calliope. Which of these words is *not* one of the words seen on the front?
    - a. Snort
    - b. Toot
    - c. Whistle
    - d. Plunk

34. ★ As you look at the giant Pete outside the big top, how many teeth does he have?
    - a. 5
    - b. 6
    - c. 4
    - d. 3

35. ★ As you stand before the Minnie Magnifique area in the side show, how many poodles are sitting on the ladder steps?
    - a. 4
    - b. 5
    - c. 6
    - d. 8

36. ★★ What is Donald Duck's part in the side show?
    - a. Hypnotist
    - b. Snake healer
    - c. Gypsy
    - d. Snake charmer

37. ★★ As you continue your tour of Storybook Circus, stop to read the banners for other acts. Which Disney character is the Pitch Perfect Prima Donna?
    - a. Lady Tremaine
    - b. Clara Cluck
    - c. Maid Marion
    - d. Clarabelle Cow

38. ★★ What talent does Humphrey the bear have in the circus?
    - a. Tight rope walker
    - b. Strong man
    - c. Unicycle
    - d. Bicycle

Did you know?

Look down at the ground as you walk along. Notice the paw prints of the various circus animals left behind around the circus grounds.

Casey Jr. Splash 'N' Soak Station

39. ★ In the center of Storybook Circus, you will find a large train car. Which circus animals are found in train car 71?
    a. Elephants
    b. Giraffes
    c. Monkeys
    d. Lions

40. ★★ How do the camels shoot water at the guests that pass by their train car?
    a. Hoses
    b. Squirt bottles
    c. Water faucets
    d. Spitting

The Barnstormer

41. ★ As you come to the entrance to The Barnstormer, what does the sign on the ticket booth read?
    a. Out to lunch
    b. Closed
    c. Out flying
    d. Come back tomorrow

42. ★★ As you come to Goofy's plane crashed into the water tower, what makes up the O on the banner hanging from the back of his plane?
    a. Bird feathers
    b. Smoke
    c. Puddle of water
    d. Propeller

43. ★ As you pass by the human cannonball take a look at the small pile of cannon balls. What common item is the top ball?
    a. Bowling ball
    b. Basketball
    c. Soccer ball
    d. Cannon ball

The Great Walt Disney World Scavenger Hunt

> **Did you know?**
>
> As you exit the Barnstormer attraction, stop and look at the back of the large Barnstormer sign above your head. On the back, you will notice the wood used is the same sign used when this attraction was the Goofy's Wiseacre Farm.

Dumbo the Flying Elephant

44. ★ As you enter the big top for Dumbo's Flying Circus, what is the name on the dog house you find?
    - a. Spike
    - b. Sport
    - c. Spot
    - d. Sprite

45. ★ How many flames do you see on the brick building in the center of the ring?
    - a. 5
    - b. 9
    - c. 7
    - d. 2

46. ★★ What type of playground equipment is the human cannonball used for?
    - a. A swing
    - b. A merry go round
    - c. Teeter Totter
    - d. A slide

Be Our Guest Restaurant

> **Did you know?**
>
> As you enter the castle and stand in the hall to give your order, listen to the suits of armor around you. Hear them speaking?

47. ★ As you enter the library to place your order, glance at the tapestries hanging above. Which Beauty & the Beast character adorns station number 3?
    a. Lumiere
    b. Cogsworth
    c. Chip
    d. Mrs. Potts

> **Did you know?**
>
> As you enter the ball room, look up at the cherubs on the ceiling fresco. The faces are the children of the animators of Beauty and the Beast. In some cases, even the animators as they looked as children.

48. ★ Enter the music box room and look around at the tapestries on the walls. What activity are Mrs. Potts and Chip engaged in?
    a. Bedtime
    b. A bath
    c. Breakfast
    d. Music lesson

49. ★★ As you look at the tapestry of Belle and Beast at the tea party, how many books are sitting on the fireplace mantle?
    a. 30
    b. 40
    c. 45
    d. 50

50. ★★★ Find the tapestry of Belle and Beast in the snow feeding the birds, how many birds do you see sitting on Beast?
    a. 15
    b. 22
    c. 18
    d. 8

> **Did you know?**
>
> As you reenter the ballroom, walk towards the large windows. Notice it is snowing outside while you dine.

The Great Walt Disney World Scavenger Hunt

Did you know?

Enter the west wing and see the beast as he looked before being cursed. You will find the bell jar with the enchanted rose within this room. Look closely at the table the bell jar sits on. The Magic Mirror sits waiting for Beast to see beyond the castle walls.

Enchanted Tales with Belle

51. ★ As you enter Belle's cottage, take a look at the décor around you. What game sits atop the table in this room?
    - a. Chess
    - b. Checkers
    - c. Ma Jong
    - d. Cards

52. ★ What color is the umbrella in the umbrella stand in the cottage?
    - a. Red
    - b. Black
    - c. Blue
    - d. Green

53. ★ As you read Belle's growth chart on the wall, what year does the tallest mark indicate?
    - a. 18 years
    - b. 16 years
    - c. 15 years
    - d. 3 years

54. ★★ You will find a large stack of books on the floor near the table. How many books do you find on this stack?
    - a. 14
    - b. 15
    - c. 20
    - d. 17

Did you know?

As you enter the workshop of Maurice, you will have the rare treat of walking through the enchanted mirror that leads to Beast's castle for an interactive story with Belle.

Gaston's Tavern

55. ★ As you approach Gaston's tavern, stop and admire the statue of Gaston and Lefou. According to the plaque at the base of this statue, who gifted this statue to the village?
    a. Maurice
    b. Beast
    c. Gaston
    d. Lefou

56. ★★ As you enter Gaston's tavern, find the dart board. How many points did Gaston score during his game?
    a. 12
    b. 60
    c. 50
    d. 6

Did you know?

You can sit in Gaston's throne like chair near the fireplace. While you rest in this magnificent seat, take a moment to bask in the glory of Gaston's painting above the fireplace.

Under the Sea – Journey of the Little Mermaid

57. ★ As you approach the queue for Under the Sea – Journey of the Little Mermaid, stop for a moment to look at the bronze plaque in front of the ship. Which of these characters is *not* seen on this plaque?
    a. Flounder
    b. Ariel
    c. Ursula
    d. King Triton

58. ★ As you walk through the queue, you will find a sign asking for your help to sort Scuttles collection. What sort of creatures need your help according to the sign?
    a. Fish
    b. Octopus
    c. Crabs
    d. Seagulls

Did you know?

As you continue through the queue, you will come across Scuttle interacting with the sea creatures. Watch as one of the creatures finds and takes the magic lamp from Aladdin.

59. ★ As your journey begins, you will find Scuttle the seagull narrating your story. What item does Scuttle have in his hands?
    a. Accordion
    b. Guitar
    c. Spyglass
    d. Storybook

60. ★★★ As you listen to Ariel's song in her collection room, how many thing-a-ma-bobs does she have?
    a. 10
    b. 30
    c. 50
    d. 20

61. ★ As you watch Ariel in her collection room, what object does Sebastian the crab pop out of?
    a. Helmet
    b. Crown
    c. Snow globe
    d. Book

62. ★ As you enter the Under the Sea party, how many tentacles does the octopus have?
    a. 6
    b. 7
    c. 8
    d. 9

63. ★★ As you pass by the fish playing drums to your right, how many fish are in the conga line?
    a. 4
    b. 5
    c. 6
    d. 7

64. ★ What instrument does the green fish play at the end of the Under the Sea party?
    a. Clarinet
    b. Saxophone
    c. Drums
    d. Flute

65. ✯✯ As you enter Ursula's lair, listen to her song. Finish this line: "I'll admit that in the past I've been a _____."
    a. Nasty
    b. Witch
    c. Stinker
    d. Pansy

66. ✯✯ As you rise out of the sea and onto land once again, what type of birds hold open the canopy for you to pass?
    a. Seagulls
    b. Doves
    c. Pelicans
    d. Cranes

67. ✯ As you watch Ariel and Prince Eric in their row boat, what color ribbon is tied in Ariel's hair?
    a. Pink
    b. Yellow
    c. Purple
    d. Blue

68. ✯ What do the ducks use for instruments as they accompany Sebastian serenading Ariel and Prince Eric?
    a. Frogs
    b. Fish
    c. Turtles
    d. Crabs

69. ✯ As you celebrate the marriage of Ariel and Prince Eric, how many lobsters do you see dancing with joy?
    a. 3
    b. 4
    c. 7
    d. 1

Pinocchio Village Haus

70. ✯✯✯ As you look around Pinocchio Village Haus, look for the mural of Pinocchio and the blue fairy. Which character is leaning on the fish bowl?
    a. Pinocchio
    b. Geppetto
    c. Figaro
    d. Cleo

71. ✯✯ As you continue your search within Pinocchio Village Haus, find the owl clock. What color is the owl clock?

a.	Brown	c.	Blue
b.	Green	d.	Red

72. ★★ Find the painting of Lampwick riding a carousel horse, what does he hold in his hand?
    a. Balloons   c. Lollypop
    b. Ice cream   d. Piece of cake

73. ★★ Look at the stained-glass window high above your head in the main room of Pinocchio Village Haus. Which marionette is 2nd from the left?
    a. Ballerina   c. Can can girl
    b. Soldier   d. Knight in Armor

Peter Pan's Flight

74. ★ Enter the queue and begin walking through the hall, stop to read the island map hanging on the wall. What is the name of the creek you see on the map?
    a. Crocodile   c. Pixie
    b. Alligator   d. Captain

Bonus Question:

75. ★★ As you enter the garden of the Banks house, you will see Mr. and Mrs. Banks in the window. What is Mrs. Banks first name?
    a. Lily   c. Mary
    b. Martha   d. Wendy

76. ★★ As you enter the children's bedroom, look out the window at Big Ben. What time is it according to this landmark?
    a. 4:55   c. 5:55
    b. 3:55   d. 6:55

77. ★★★ Find the wall calendar within the children's bedroom. What date is circled on the calendar?
    a. December 27
    b. December 25
    c. January 27
    d. November 27

78. ★ On the nightstand, you will find several books held in place by an elephant. What color is this elephant bookend?
    a. Green
    b. Gray
    c. Pink
    d. Blue

> ### Did you know?
> As you walk around the children's bedroom watch for Tinkerbell interacting with the toy boat and spinning the globe while she investigates the items throughout the room. Later you will see her bump into a painting and looking at herself in the mirror.

> ### Did you know?
> Watch for the shadows on the wall of the children's bedroom. Reach up and ring the bells with your hand's shadow or play with the butterflies that appear randomly during your time in the nursery.

79. ★★★ As you enter your ride vehicle to fly to Neverland, which of these dolls sits at the tea table in the children's bedroom?
    a. Mickey Mouse
    b. Tinkerbell
    c. Mrs. Beasley
    d. Raggedy Anne

80. ★★★ As you come to Neverland and see the lost boys sitting at the campfire, which of these is *not* one of their costumes?
    a. Skunk
    b. Bear
    c. Deer
    d. Fox

The Great Walt Disney World Scavenger Hunt

81. ★★ As you come to the Indian village, how many Indians do you see?
    a. 6
    b. 7
    c. 4
    d. 9

82. ★★ As we see Captain Hook for the last time, what word do you hear him yell out?
    a. "Help me Mr. Smee!"
    b. "Pan!"
    c. "Tink!"
    d. "No!"

83. ★ As you exit your ride vehicle notice the mushrooms to your left. How many are there?
    a. 10
    b. 15
    c. 12
    d. 9

It's a Small World

84. ★ As you approach the queue for It's a Small World, how many children do you see in the boat above the entrance?
    a. 14
    b. 15
    c. 12
    d. 13

85. ★ As you see the It's a Small World clock across from the queue, which of these numbers is at the top on the right?
    a. 7
    b. 3
    c. 2
    d. 12

86. ★ As you enter your ride vehicle and begin your journey, finish this quote above the archway to this attraction, "Welcome to the happiest cruise that ever _____."
    a. Way
    b. Sailed
    c. Was
    d. Floated

87. ★★ As you approach England, how many of the wooden soldiers are playing the drums?

a.	9	c.	3
b.	6	d.	12

88. ★ In the Spain scene, what does Don Quixote stab at with his lance?
    a. A windmill
    b. A bull
    c. A piñata
    d. A fountain

89. ★★ What shape are the pendulums of the cuckoo clocks in Switzerland?
    a. Hearts
    b. Circles
    c. Stars
    d. Triangles

90. ★ As you watch the kites above you in china, which animal is depicted on the green kite?
    a. Dragon
    b. Bear
    c. Owl
    d. Camel

91. ★★ How many arms does the goddess statue in Thailand have?
    a. 2
    b. 6
    c. 8
    d. 4

92. ★ What color is the elephant in the African continent scene?
    a. Yellow
    b. Blue
    c. Grey
    d. Pink

93. ★★★ As you continue cruising through Africa, how many dancers with red feathers do you see?
    a. 6
    b. 10
    c. 8
    d. 12

94. ★★ As you enter South America, what do the penguins wear on their heads?
    a. Feathers
    b. Sombreros
    c. Flowers
    d. Top Hats

95. ★ What musical instrument does the cactus play in South America?
    a. Guitar
    b. Maracas
    c. Tambourine
    d. Banjo

96. ★ What color is the kangaroo you encounter in Australia?
    a. Blue
    b. Pink
    c. Yellow
    d. Green

97. ★★ As you have been enjoying your cruise around the world, finish this line from the *It's a Small World* song, "It's a world of laughter, a world of tears, a world of hope and a world of _____."
    a. Clears
    b. Deer's
    c. Gears
    d. Fears

98. ★★ As you finish your cruise, what does the word on the inside of the sun to your left read?
    a. Aloha
    b. Adios
    c. Goodbye
    d. Sayonara

Tangled area

> **Did you know?**
>
> As you wander through the small corner of Fantasyland, take a look at the horseshoe prints on the ground. Notice the name Maximus at the top of each horseshoe print. These are the horseshoes of the captain of the guard that chased Flynn Rider in the film *Tangled*.

99. ★★ Look at the reward poster for Vladimir near the restrooms. What will be served with the tea according to this poster?
    a. Grog
    b. Finger Sandwiches
    c. Fingers
    d. Peanut Butter and Jelly

100. ★ According to the wanted poster for Hookhand, why is he back by popular demand?
    a. He paid them
    b. His gang requested
    c. Flynn Rider asked
    d. He insisted

> ### Did you know?
> Just before you enter the ladies' room in the Tangled area of Fantasyland, look at the icon on the small sign to the left of the doorway. The icon has long blonde hair just like Princess Rapunzel. Also, look above the doorway and you will see that Rapunzel has been hard at work painting the stones.

101. ★ If you enter the men's restroom, which of these is *not* one of the captured villains on the wall?
    a. Rapunzel
    b. Flynn Rider
    c. Shorty
    d. The Stabbington Brothers

> ### Did you know?
> Look carefully around the Tangled area and you will find a sack of apples sitting atop a wooden crate. Notice one of the apples has a large bite taken out of it. These apples are a gift from Flynn Rider to Maximus and a nod to the end of *Tangled* in which Flynn tosses Maximus this very sack of apples.

Liberty Square

Go back in time to the days of the colonies where you can explore an island out of a classic story by Mark Twain, spend some time with the presidents of our United States past and present or expand your knowledge of the moments that make up the history of the United States of America.

Liberty Square Riverboat

1. ★★ According to the plaque at the entrance to Liberty Square, what did the colonists declare their independence from?
   a. Slavery
   b. England
   c. Tyranny
   d. Taxation

2. ★★ As you are getting ready to cast off on the Liberty Square Riverboat, what does the captain say to secure?
   a. All passengers
   b. Rigging
   c. All cargo
   d. All stock

3. ★★ As you hear your captain begin your journey, what is his name?
   a. Mark Twain
   b. Horace Bixby
   c. Walt Disney
   d. Samuel Clemens

4. ★★ How many voyages has Sam Clemens been on according to your captain?
   a. 100
   b. 200
   c. 500
   d. 110

5. ★★ As your captain shares his knowledge about Frontierland, how does he describe himself as a boy growing up on the riverbank?
   a. Wet foot
   b. Stocking foot
   c. Hot foot
   d. Barefoot

6. ★★ What is the name of the pond on Tom Sawyer island?
   a. Potters
   b. Huck Finns
   c. Becky Thatcher
   d. Millers

7. ★★ What do the natives call the hot springs according to your captain?
   a. Friendly spirits
   b. Unfriendly spirits
   c. Friendly water sprites
   d. Unfriendly geysers

8. ★★ What is the name of the Indian tribe you see by the bank of the river?
   a. Hopi
   b. Black foot
   c. Powhatan
   d. Cherokee

9. ★★ Why is cutthroat corner named as such?
   a. Pirates
   b. Indians
   c. Thieves
   d. Stabbington Brothers

The Hall of Presidents

> **Did you know?**
>
> As you enter the waiting area for the Hall of Presidents, you will see the Great Seal of the United States in rug form surrounded by a low rail. This is the only other place in the world besides Washington D.C. it is used. This took an act of congress for Walt Disney World to be given permission to use the seal.

10. ★★★ As you walk through the museum before entering the theater, you will find several quotes throughout the room written in gold. Complete the following quote, "I've always been a kind of a _____ American. I think I get that red, white and blue streak up and down my back every once in a while."
    a. Flag waving
    b. Quiet
    c. Boisterous
    d. Billboard

11. ★★ As you explore the foyer of the Hall of Presidents, find the bust of Abraham Lincoln near the curtains. In which year did Walt Disney create the Abraham Lincoln attraction for the New York World's Fair?
    a. 1964
    b. 1965
    c. 1864
    d. 1865

12. ★★ As you enter the theater and the show begins, listen to the narrator talk about the origins of our country. According to your narrator, how many years did the revolutionary war last?
    a. 6
    b. 18
    c. 80
    d. 8

13. ★★★ When General George Washington retired from military service, he retired to his home. Where was his home located?
    a. Washington D.C.
    b. Tacoma
    c. Mount Vernon
    d. Georgetown

14. ★★ As you hear your narrator talk about the different men would become president in the early years, they referred to the presidency as a "glorious _____."
    a. Burden
    b. Democracy
    c. Stronghold
    d. Right

15. ★★ When Abraham Lincoln is elected the 16th President of the United States, where does your narrator state he was from originally?
    a. Indiana
    b. Idaho
    c. Illinois
    d. Iowa

16. ★★ At the beginning of the civil war, how many states seceded from the union?
    a. 10
    b. 12
    c. 8
    d. 11

17. ★★★ What was the purpose of Lincoln's Gettysburg Address given on November 19, 1863?
    a. Dedicate a cemetery
    b. Abolish slavery
    c. Run for a second term
    d. End the civil war

18. ★★ President Theodore Roosevelt borrows a line from an African proverb, "Speak softly and carry a _____."
    a. Large weapon
    b. Big stick
    c. Loaded pistol
    d. Small stone

The Great Walt Disney World Scavenger Hunt

19. ★★ As you watch the large screen, a newspaper headline appears with the words "Lost in New" printed, what is the date on this newspaper?
    a. October 28, 1929
    b. October 29, 1928
    c. October 31, 1929
    d. November 28, 1929

20. ★★ What disease crippled President Franklin D. Roosevelt?
    a. Polio
    b. Measles
    c. Shingles
    d. Cancer

Bonus Question

21. ★★★ As you listen to the names of our presidents being called out, how many have been direct family members?
    a. 6
    b. 45
    c. 12
    d. 4

22. ★★★ As you listen to the oath of office recited by our current President, Donald J. Trump, how many words are there in the oath?
    a. 12
    b. 300
    c. 35
    d. 50

23. ★★★ Which of our nation's songs can be heard as you exit the hall of presidents?
    a. "The Star-Spangled Banner"
    b. "The Battle Hymn of the Republic"
    c. "America the Beautiful"
    d. "God Bless America"

---

24. ★★★ As you walk through Liberty Square, look at the ground beneath you. What is the brown strip of ground running through the cement walkway representing?

a. Dirt
b. Waste
c. Water
d. Road

> ### Did you know?
> There is a wooden stockade near the entrance to the riverboat attraction where you can put your head and arms through to take pictures. This is representative of the way criminals were punished by putting them on display for the townsfolk to ridicule.

The Haunted Mansion

25. ★★ As you enter the queue for the Haunted Mansion you will find several graves stone with the busts of family members who have died. As you read the epitaphs, what is the emblem on the epitaph of Aunt Florence?
    a. Hammer
    b. Car
    c. Gun
    d. Bottle

26. ★★ What animal adorns the headstone of Bertie?
    a. Owl
    b. Spider
    c. Crow
    d. Snake

27. ★★★ What kind of eyewear does uncle Jacob wear on his headstone?
    a. Monocle
    b. Glasses
    c. Opera Glasses
    d. Binoculars

28. ★ Continue your way into the cemetery and find the large monument for the sea captain. According to the epitaph for the captain, how did he die?
    a. At sea
    b. An octopus
    c. In brine
    d. Taking a bath

The Great Walt Disney World Scavenger Hunt

> ### Did you know?
> If you stand near the captain's grave, you will get sprayed with water periodically. Listen for the captain to sneeze just before getting sprayed.

> ### Did you know?
> As you make your way around the cemetery, touch the instruments on the sides of the large crypt. Each one will play as if you are playing the instrument yourself.

29. ★ In the center of the cemetery you will find the grave of Master Gracey, finish his epitaph, "No _____ please at his request."
    a. Laughing
    b. Crying
    c. Mourning
    d. Flowers

> ### Did you know?
> As you approach the front doors of the Haunted Mansion, you will find the grave of Madam Leota on the hill to your left. Her eyes open periodically to stare at you as you walk by.

30. ★★ As you enter the mansion and step into the gallery, what does your ghost host say about the guest in their mortal state?
    a. Evil
    b. Corruptible
    c. Genuine
    d. Adorable

31. ★ As you watch the portraits around you stretch, what does the label on the dynamite say?
    a. Danger
    b. Warning
    c. No Flame
    d. Kaboom

> ### Did you know?
> Listen carefully as you exit the stretching portrait gallery, can you hear the ghosts telling you to move forward?

32. ✯✯✯ As you enter your doom buggies and begin your journey, take a close look at the portraits lining the walls. What does the woman lying on the couch hold in her hand when the lightning strikes?
    a. Fan
    b. Toy
    c. Goblet
    d. Bone

33. ✯✯ As you enter the library, the walls are lined with first editions, only what kind of books according to your ghost host?
    a. Classics
    b. Ghost stories
    c. Love stories
    d. Witch tales

34. ✯✯ Complete the following your ghost host tells you, "Hot and cold running_____."
    a. Chills
    b. Thrills
    c. Water
    d. Ghosts

35. ✯✯ Madam Leota chants in her trance, finish this line she utters, "Give us a hint by ringing a _____."
    a. Spell
    b. Knell
    c. Bell
    d. Swell

36. ✯✯ As you enter the dining room, how many candles appear on the birthday cake the ghost blows out at her party?
    a. 10
    b. 23
    c. 13
    d. 4

The Great Walt Disney World Scavenger Hunt

37. ★ You will encounter the bride in the attic, what does she hold in her hand as she speaks to you?
    a. Hammer
    b. Shovel
    c. Bouquet
    d. Axe

> **Did you know?**
>
> As you work your way through the attic, take notice of the pearls the bride wears in each picture. Each time the bride married, another strand of pearls is added to her neck.

38. ★★ Listen to the ghosts sing as you make your way through the cemetery. Finish this line, "Don't close your eyes and don't try to hide, for a _____ spook may sit by your side."
    a. Scary
    b. Silly
    c. Floating
    d. Terrifying

39. ★★ As you enter the graveyard scene, you will see the ghost band playing, which of these is *not* one of the instruments being played?
    a. Bagpipes
    b. Lyre
    c. Xylophone
    d. Guitar

40. ★ As you approach the singing busts, how many of these statues have bowties?
    a. 4
    b. 3
    c. 6
    d. 5

41. ★★ As you enter the crypt, you will see the famous hitchhiking ghosts. What does the smallest ghost hold in his hand?
    a. Suitcase
    b. Trowel
    c. Hat
    d. Ball and chain

42. ★ As you exit the Haunted Mansion attraction, stop for a moment to read the crypts. What does the inscription in the upper right corner read?
    a. MT Tomb
    b. IM Ready
    c. CU Later
    d. Asher T Ashes

Did you know?

As you exit the Haunted Mansion, you will see a small pet cemetery above you. Look closely and you will see a homage to Mr. Toad on this hillside.

43. ★★ As you walk through Liberty Square you will find the Liberty Tree. According to the plaque, what was its proudest moment?
    a. Repeal of the Stamp Act
    b. Boston tea party
    c. End of the Revolutionary War
    d. Washington's inauguration

Did you know?

If you look very carefully at the windows in Liberty Square you will find two lanterns sitting on the frame of one of the windows. This is a homage to the famous poem Paul Revere's Ride, with two lanterns indicating the British would come by sea to attack the colonies.

Adventureland

Take some time to explore the far-off exotic places Adventureland has to offer. Investigate the jungle or explore a temple. Only the limits of your imagination will hold you back from the adventure around the next corner.

1. ★ As you enter through the gates of Adventureland, take a look at the post of the Adventureland sign. How many skeleton skulls to do you on the sign?
   a. 5   c. 13
   b. 12   d. 8

Did you know?

This area of Walt Disney World was opened in 1973 when the imagineers realized the immense success of the Adventureland at Disneyland resort.

Swiss Family Robinson Treehouse

2. ★★ As you begin your exploration of the Swiss Family Robinson Treehouse, find the carving made by Franz giving guests some information as to how the family came

to this island. In what year did the Robinson family land and establish their treehouse according to the inscription written by Franz?

    a. 1871   c. 1805
    b. 1855   d. 1971

3. ★ As you continue to read the inscription, what is the name of the ship they were on when they were shipwrecked?

    a. Swiss   c. Toucan
    b. Elias   d. Swallow

4. ★ As you come to the dining room, what book do you see sitting on top of the table in the center of the room?

    a. Bible   c. Dictionary
    b. Telephone directory   d. Robinson Crusoe

5. ★ Look up at the rafters above in the dining room. What does the small barrel contain according to the writing on it?

    a. Milk   c. Rum
    b. Water   d. Brandy

6. ★ At the jungle lookout, what does the Robinson family often pause to reflect on?

    a. Whether they would get rescued   c. The food supply
    b. The weather   d. Our small world

7. ★ In the library, you will find a map on the side table. What item do you find with it?

    a. Weather almanac   c. Accounting ledger
    b. Ships log   d. Household inventory

8. ★ As you come upon the kitchen area of the treehouse, what is the sink made from?

a.	Coconut shell	c.	Hollow log
b.	Seashell	d.	Bucket

Walt Disney's Enchanted Tiki Room

9. ★★★ As you enter the theater and take your seat, the birds will wake up and begin speaking. Which of these names is *not* one of the hosts of the Enchanted Tiki Room?
   a. Frederick   c. Fritz
   b. Jose   d. Pierre

10. ★★ According to the song, if the birds were not in the show, where would they be?
    a. Out the Door   c. Flying away
    b. In the audience d. Riding the tea cups

11. ★★ According to your Emcee, what is Fritz missing?
    a. Feathers   c. Hair
    b. Wings   d. Tail

12. ★★★ Which of these is *not* one of the names of the white birds on the bird mobile?
    a. Collette   c. Gigi
    b. Fifi   d. Juanita

13. ★★★ Jose wonders aloud what happened to which bird?
    a. Rosita   c. Maria
    b. Juanita   d. Tatiana

14. ★★ When the rain begins, what does Fritz say has been left running?
    a. The shower   c. The faucet
    b. The hose   d. The river

15. ★★ When the thunder begins, who do the birds say is angered by all the celebrating?

a. The volcano
   b. The tikis
   c. The gods
   d. The birds

16. ★★ What famous Disney song is heard as you exit the Enchanted Tiki Room?
    a. "Zip A Dee Do Dah"
    b. "Mickey Mouse Club"
    c. "Heigh Ho"
    d. "It's a Small World"

Jungle Cruise

17. ★★ As you enter the queue for The Jungle Cruise, read some of the notices in the glass case. What does the notice for Malaria say to keep in your supplies?
    a. Antibiotics
    b. Mosquito netting
    c. Quinine
    d. Bug spray

18. ★★★ As you look at the items in the wire storage area at the beginning of the queue, stop to look at some of the items. What kind of salt is in the small blue container?
    a. Table salt
    b. Sea salt
    c. Leech salt
    d. Kosher salt

19. ★ As you read the torn shirt found in the queue, what are they giving away for free?
    a. Dogs
    b. Elephants
    c. Tigers
    d. Kittens

20. ★★ As you continue through the queue for The Jungle Cruise, find the red sign. What does it warn against using the boats for?
    a. Joy Riding down the Congo
    b. Daredevil trips over Schweitzer Falls
    c. Crocodile Racing
    d. Gorilla Hunting

The Great Walt Disney World Scavenger Hunt

> **Did you know?**
>
> If you look at the cage with the tarantula, don't get too close or you might lose a finger.

21. ★★ As you continue through The Jungle Cruise queue, what does the Field & Co. deal with besides spices?
    a. Monkey Fur
    b. Ivory
    c. Rum
    d. Exotic animals

22. ★★ As you approach the loading dock, read the crew menu board. What is on the menu for Friday?
    a. Giant stag beetle
    b. Chicken (really)
    c. Three toed skink
    d. Rock python

23. ★ As you enter the boat and begin your cruise, you will come to the large native boats to your right, what do you see perched atop the poles?
    a. Birds
    b. Coconuts
    c. Skulls
    d. Animal Hides

24. ★★ What species of snake do you see coiled in the tree as you pass by?
    a. Cobra
    b. Rattlesnake
    c. King snake
    d. Python

25. ★ What color is the jeep you see in the camp the gorillas have taken over?
    a. Blue
    b. Green
    c. Yellow
    d. Pink

26. ★ As you pass the African belt, how many lions do you see?
    a. 4
    b. 8
    c. 6
    d. 12

27. ☆ As you pass by the safari party stuck on the pole, what creatures are watching from below?
    a. Hyena
    b. Monkeys
    c. Wolves
    d. Hippo

28. ☆☆ What is the name of Smiley the crocodile's girlfriend according to your skipper?
    a. Amber
    b. Ginger
    c. MaryAnn
    d. Mrs. Howell

29. ☆☆ According to your skipper, who were the falls named after?
    a. Albert Schweitzer
    b. Albert Falls
    c. Albert Einstein
    d. Albert Brooks

30. ☆ As you enter the hippo pool, how do you know the hippos are about to attack, according to your skipper?
    a. Wiggling their ears
    b. Roaring
    c. Shooting a pistol
    d. Singing

31. ☆ As you approach the native camp, what items are stacked inside the canoe at the river edge?
    a. Paddles
    b. Spears
    c. Skulls
    d. Shields

32. ☆ As you pass the native village, what do the ambush party hold in their hands?
    a. Blow guns
    b. Daggers
    c. Pistols
    d. Spears

33. ☆☆ As you come to the elephant bathing pool, why is it ok to take pictures according to your skipper?
    a. You have a permit
    b. No one is looking
    c. They have their trunks on
    d. Drawings take too long

The Great Walt Disney World Scavenger Hunt

> **Did you know?**
> If you look at the cage with the tarantula, don't get too close or you might lose a finger.

21. ★★ As you continue through The Jungle Cruise queue, what does the Field & Co. deal with besides spices?
    a. Monkey Fur
    b. Ivory
    c. Rum
    d. Exotic animals

22. ★★ As you approach the loading dock, read the crew menu board. What is on the menu for Friday?
    a. Giant stag beetle
    b. Chicken (really)
    c. Three toed skink
    d. Rock python

23. ★ As you enter the boat and begin your cruise, you will come to the large native boats to your right, what do you see perched atop the poles?
    a. Birds
    b. Coconuts
    c. Skulls
    d. Animal Hides

24. ★★ What species of snake do you see coiled in the tree as you pass by?
    a. Cobra
    b. Rattlesnake
    c. King snake
    d. Python

25. ★ What color is the jeep you see in the camp the gorillas have taken over?
    a. Blue
    b. Green
    c. Yellow
    d. Pink

26. ★ As you pass the African belt, how many lions do you see?
    a. 4
    b. 8
    c. 6
    d. 12

27. ★ As you pass by the safari party stuck on the pole, what creatures are watching from below?
    a. Hyena
    b. Monkeys
    c. Wolves
    d. Hippo

28. ★★ What is the name of Smiley the crocodile's girlfriend according to your skipper?
    a. Amber
    b. Ginger
    c. MaryAnn
    d. Mrs. Howell

29. ★★ According to your skipper, who were the falls named after?
    a. Albert Schweitzer
    b. Albert Falls
    c. Albert Einstein
    d. Albert Brooks

30. ★ As you enter the hippo pool, how do you know the hippos are about to attack, according to your skipper?
    a. Wiggling their ears
    b. Roaring
    c. Shooting a pistol
    d. Singing

31. ★ As you approach the native camp, what items are stacked inside the canoe at the river edge?
    a. Paddles
    b. Spears
    c. Skulls
    d. Shields

32. ★ As you pass the native village, what do the ambush party hold in their hands?
    a. Blow guns
    b. Daggers
    c. Pistols
    d. Spears

33. ★★ As you come to the elephant bathing pool, why is it ok to take pictures according to your skipper?
    a. You have a permit
    b. No one is looking
    c. They have their trunks on
    d. Drawings take too long

The Great Walt Disney World Scavenger Hunt

34. ★ As you reach the end of the tour, what is Trader Sam trying to sell you?
    a. An Elephant
    b. Necklaces
    c. Shrunken heads
    d. Spears

35. ★ As you exit the Jungle Cruise, what did the broken cage once contain?
    a. Orangutan
    b. Gorilla
    c. Zebra
    d. Chimpanzee

36. ★★★ Which of these is *not* one of the rivers you explore on the Jungle Cruise?
    a. Amazon
    b. Ganges
    c. Nile
    d. Congo

37. ★ Before you finish your adventure on the Jungle Cruise, take a look at the green chalkboard to your right as you exit your boat. Of the missing boats, what is the name of the fifth boat on the list?
    a. Fateless Fiona
    b. Los Lucia
    c. Sunken Sonia
    d. Run aground Sue

38. ★ Of the list of missing persons on the green chalkboard, what is the name of the fourth person listed?
    a. Ilene Dover
    b. Emma Boylen
    c. C.M. Cooken
    d. Albert Knot

39. ★★ Read the black board with the names of missing persons. Which of these is *not* one of the names listed?
    a. Seymore Butz
    b. Ilene Dover
    c. C.M. Cooken
    d. Betty Dunt

> ### Did you know?
> Read some of the crates around you. You will find some very amusing quips around the edges of the crates. The upside-down crate with "handle with care" printed, note just below the message "Who's kidding who? Contents probably already broken."
>
> Find the box with "this end up" printed on each of the four sides or the Quicksand box with RUSH stamped across the side.

Pirates of the Caribbean

40. ★ As you begin your cruise, what does the disembodied voice say. "Dead men _____."
    a. Have no tales
    b. Tell no tales
    c. Don't tell fairytales
    d. Say nothing

> ### Did you know?
> Look at the rock formation to your left just before the beach scene. You will see a skull formed into the rock.

41. ★ How many skeletons do you see on the beach to your left?
    a. 4
    b. 6
    c. 7
    d. 5

42. ★★★ As you travel to the war between the pirate ship and the fortress, what is the name of the pirate ship?
    a. The Wicked Wench
    b. The Black Pearl
    c. The Flying Dutchman
    d. The Columbia

43. ★★ As you watch the scene with the villager being dunked in the well, what is the name of this man?

| a. | Jose | c. | Jack |
| b. | Carlos | d. | Manuel |

44. ★★ In the auction scene, what does the auctioneer tell the woman to show the bidders?
    - a. Her flock
    - b. Her hens
    - c. Her chicks
    - d. Her birds

45. ★★ What does the redhead tell the auctioneer they want?
    - a. Gold
    - b. Jewels
    - c. Treasure
    - d. Rum

46. ★ What does the last man in line have strapped to his back for the auction?
    - a. A harp
    - b. A piano
    - c. A grandfather clock
    - d. A table

47. ★ How many pigs do you see in the mud with the sleeping pirate?
    - a. 4
    - b. 5
    - c. 2
    - d. 3

48. ★★ As you enter the jail cell scene, which of these is *not* one of the ways the pirates try to lure the dog with the key?
    - a. A bone
    - b. A dog biscuit
    - c. A rope
    - d. Whistling

Frontierland

Go back to the days of the wild west and explore the roots of America with the settlers who started this great country. Take a wild ride on a runaway mine train or get up close and personal with live animals as you explore the origins of the United States.

For those looking for a thrill, join Brer Rabbit on his adventures through Splash Mountain.

Country Bear Jamboree

1. ★ As you enter the theater and see the three animal heads on the wall, which of these is not one of the names of the heads?
    a. Bill
    b. Buff
    c. Max
    d. Melvin

2. ★★ If you read the advertisements on the stage before the show starts, what item is currently on sale?
    a. Coon skin hats
    b. Hunting rifles
    c. Fur coats
    d. Taxidermy

3. ★★ As you continue reading the advertisements, what is the name of the realty office?
    a. Hibernators
    b. Beehive
    c. Honey Bee
    d. Humphrey's

The Great Walt Disney World Scavenger Hunt

4. ☆ As you listen to Henry sing the first song, which musical key is the song in?
   a. Key of C
   b. Key of A
   c. Key of G
   d. Key of D

5. ☆☆ According to the song *Momma don't whoop little Beauford*, what do the singers suggest she do instead?
   a. Hang him
   b. Drown him
   c. Tie him up
   d. Shoot him

6. ☆ What animal sings with Henry when he sings *The Ballad of Davey Crockett*?
   a. Rabbit
   b. Raccoon
   c. Bear
   d. Buffalo

---

7. ☆☆ As you walk the streets of Frontierland, you will come upon a red barrel. What is the name of the fire chief whose name is written on this barrel?
   a. Walt Disney
   b. J.M. Barrie
   c. P.J. Hogan
   d. Richard Le Pere Jr.

8. ☆ As you walk through Frontierland, find the wanted poster with the rope around the picture, how much is the reward for capturing this criminal?
   a. $300.00
   b. $30.00
   c. $10.00
   d. $3,000.00

Frontierland Shooting Gallery

9. ☆☆ As you look at the tombstones in the Frontierland Shooting Gallery, what symbol appears on Nancy Dans grave?
   a. Gun
   b. Arrow
   c. Heart
   d. Star

10. ✯✯ What did Ol' Tom Hubbard die with according to his tombstone?
    a. Smile
    b. Frown
    c. Scowl
    d. Smirk

11. ✯ What item do you see sticking out of A. Carpenter's grave?
    a. A hammer
    b. A T-square
    c. A chisel
    d. A saw

12. ✯✯ As you continue on your way through Frontierland, you will see a notice for the horse auctions, according to this notice, how many head of choice stock are there?
    a. 45
    b. 30
    c. 35
    d. 135

Splash Mountain

13. ✯ As you enter the doors for the barn at Splash Mountain, how many feet tall is the plunge according to the notice on the door?
    a. 50 feet
    b. 40 feet
    c. 60 feet
    d. 500 feet

14. ✯ As you enter the barn, what is the name on the wooden box to your left?
    a. Chester
    b. Chilacoffee
    c. Chesapeake
    d. Chickenfeed

15. ✯ How many eggs do you see on the straw to the left just inside the barn entrance to Splash Mountain?
    a. 8
    b. 7
    c. 9
    d. 19

The Great Walt Disney World Scavenger Hunt

16. ★★ As you pass the sign post in the queue, which of these is *not* one of the names listed?
    a. Br'er Rabbit   c. Br'er Bear
    b. Br'er Turtle   d. Br'er Bird

17. ★ As you walk through the cave in the queue, which animals house do you pass by?
    a. Br'er Fox   c. Br'er Rabbit
    b. Br'er Frog   d. Br'er Bird

18. ★ As you enter your log and begin your journey, you will pass by a covered wagon, what do they sell according to the writing on the tarp?
    a. Critter Comfort   c. Critter Potion
    b. Critter Trumpet   d. Critter Elixir

19. ★★ You will pass by a moonshine jug on your right, which critter makes this?
    a. Chipmunk   c. Muskrat
    b. Gopher   d. Otter

20. ★ As you enter the mountain, what activity does the sign say you cannot do?
    a. No fishing   c. No splashing
    b. No laughing   d. No dancing

21. ★ What musical instrument do you see the raccoon playing on the riverbank?
    a. Drums   c. Tuba
    b. Guitar   d. Harmonica

22. ★ What kind of animal is sitting on the top of the fishing alligator as they sing about the laughing place?
    a. Turtle
    b. Frog
    c. Bird
    d. Lizard

23. ★★ As you start the climb to Br'er Foxes lair, what type of bird is talking to you from the tree branch above?
    a. Eagles
    c. Vultures
    b. Hawks
    d. Ostriches

24. ★★ As you approach the river boat where the animals are singing, which animal is playing the organ?
    a. Horse
    c. Cow
    b. Goat
    d. Pig

25. ★★ As you exit Splash Mountain, stop and look at the bird house made from acorns. What is painted on the mail box in front of this little house?
    a. Confederate flag
    c. American flag
    b. Mickey Mouse
    d. Goofy

Did you know?

The concept for Splash Mountain is from the classic film *Song of the South*. This film, released in 1946, was the story of Uncle Remus and the stories he told the children about Br'er Fox, Br'er Bear and Br'er Rabbit. While the DVD was never released in the United States, it remains a classic to die hard Disney enthusiasts.

Briar Patch

26. ★ As you enter The Briar Patch shop, at the entrance to Splash Mountain, stop and take a look at the sampler hanging from the chimney. Which of these words adorn this sampler?
    a. Briar sweet briar
    c. Cave sweet cave
    b. Home sweet home
    d. Splash sweet Splash

The Great Walt Disney World Scavenger Hunt

Bonus Question:

27. ✯✯✯ Look at the bunny house above you. Find the framed painting in the room with the rocking chair. What is the name of this famous painting?
    a. Mona Lisa
    b. Whistler's Mother
    c. American Gothic
    d. Bunny Mother

28. ✯✯✯ As you look in the kitchen of the bunny house, what is the time on the clock sitting on the shelf?
    a. 12:18
    b. 2:18
    c. 3:18
    d. 1:18

29. ✯ Find the framed picture of the bunny family. How many bunnies do you see in this picture?
    a. 6
    b. 7
    c. 8
    d. 9

Did you know?

If you look at the shelves behind the counter you will find a nondescript barrel with the word laughs painted on it. This is literally a Barrel of Laughs.

Walt Disney Railroad Frontierland Station

30. ✯ As you make your way to the station platform, stop for a moment to read the wanted posters. How much is the reward for the Younger brothers?
    a. $10,000.00
    b. $15,000.00
    c. $25,000.00
    d. $15.00

31. ✯ What is Curly McKay wanted for according to his poster?
    a. Cattle rustling
    b. Murder
    c. Train robbery
    d. Armed stagecoach robbery

32. ★★ Find the train schedule on the chalk board. From which city is engine 55 arriving?
    a. San Francisco
    b. Red Bluff
    c. Big Thunder
    d. Tucson

33. ★★ As you pass by the stove, what is written on the front?
    a. Frontierland Railroad
    b. Walt Disney World
    c. Red Cross Oak
    d. Santa Fe Railroad

34. ★ As you pass the Baggage and Freight office, look around at the items within. Finish the label on the box, "Adams March of _____."
    a. Republic
    b. Democracy
    c. Capitalism
    d. Dimes

Did you know?

As you exit the Frontierland Railroad station, stop and look at the wanted poster for Frank and Jessie James. Note that someone has crossed out the alive part of the poster.

Big Thunder Mountain Railroad

35. ★★ According to the sign of the town of Big Thunder, was is the population today?
    a. 38
    b. 247
    c. 138
    d. 2015

36. ★★ As you enter the queue, you will see a wagon with mining supplies. What is the name on this wagon?
    a. Disneydale
    b. Clarksville
    c. Clarkdale
    d. Frontierdale

The Great Walt Disney World Scavenger Hunt

37. ★★ As you continue through the queue, you will see a sign with a list of things you cannot do. Which of these is *not* one of the items listed?
    a. Gum chewing
    b. Drinking
    c. Fighting
    d. Whistling

38. ★★★ As you pass the paymaster window, what item do you need to drop at the end of your shift?
    a. Pick
    b. Tag
    c. Card
    d. Gold

39. ★★ Find the pay rates schedule. What is the daily pay allowance for a shaftsman according to this chart?
    a. 10.84
    b. 2.47
    c. 2.38
    d. 2.26

40. ★★★ Which President of the United States signed the Mineral and Land grant issued to Barnabus T. Bullion?
    a. John Tyler
    b. Zachary Taylor
    c. Millard Filmore
    d. James K. Polk

41. ★★ Find the red sign informing miners that they are required to bunk at the Big Thunder Boarding House. How often are baths provided according to this sign?
    a. Daily
    b. Weekly
    c. Monthly
    d. As needed

42. ★★ According to the assay report, what is the condition of the Tumbleweed Tunnel?
    a. Flash flood
    b. Unknown
    c. Open
    d. Avalanche

43. ★★ According to the assay report, how deep is the Bat Cave?
    a. 1,690 feet
    b. 400 feet
    c. 700 feet
    d. 4,850 feet

Catherine F. Olen

44. ★★★ Find the wanted poster for the Hash Knife Outfit. Which of these is *not* one of the reasons this gang are wanted?
    a. Bungling
    b. Cow punching
    c. Tomfoolery
    d. Chicanery

Did you know?

Find the telegram pinned to the board addressed to the sheriff of Tumbleweed. The telegram talks about Theodore Ogelvie and Amos Tucker heading your way. This telegram is a reference to the classic Disney feature film *The Apple Dumpling Gang* starring Tim Conway and Don Knotts in the parts of these two bandits.

---

45. ★★★ Find the letter from Eberhardt to the Professor. What came back with a vengeance after Eberhardt tried his miracle elixir?
    a. Bursitis
    b. Bunions
    c. Warts
    d. Halitosis

46. ★★ Find the advertisement for Boothill Layaway. According to their prices, how much extra are mourners at your funeral?
    a. $30.00
    b. $10.00
    c. $ 42.00
    d. $5.00

47. ★★★ As you continue working your way through the mining operation, you will find a small note on the wall with a drawing of two buffalo. According to this note, wounds, illnesses and missing limbs are not excuses for what?
    a. Moving back home
    b. Extra pay
    c. Missing a work shift
    d. Laziness

48. ★★ On this wall you will find a note written by Spike looking for a new roommate. According to this note,

he is looking for someone who does not smoke or
_____.
- a. Eat beans
- b. Chews tobacco
- c. Keeps a pet skunk
- d. Steals food

49. ★ As you begin your ride, what does the prospector tell you "This here's the wildest ride in the _____."
    - a. West
    - b. Forest
    - c. Mine
    - d. Wilderness

---

50. ★ In what year was the Frontierland town hall founded?
    - a. 1876
    - b. 1976
    - c. 1867
    - d. 1970

51. ★★★ Outside of Pecos Bill Tall Tale Inn you will find a notice for Herrick's Vegetable Pills. Which of the symptoms listed is *not* one of the items Herrick's cures?
    - a. Worms
    - b. Head lice
    - c. Sick headache
    - d. Dyspepsia

Tom Sawyer Island

52. ★★ As you arrive on Tom Sawyer Island, read the note left by Tom. who was more scared than he was on the island according to the note?
    - a. Becky
    - b. Huck
    - c. Joe
    - d. Aunt Polly

53. ★★ As you approach Harper's Mill, what does the sign ask you not to scare?
    - a. The millers
    - b. The mice
    - c. Huck Finn
    - d. The birds

54. ★ As you enter Old Scratches Mystery Mine, what does the sign advise you *not* to do?
    a. Dig
    b. Whistle
    c. Stop
    d. Run

55. ★★ As you enter the fort, what do they call the area that is used for lookout with rifles?
    a. Rifle Roost
    b. Rifle Roof
    c. Rifle Lookout
    d. Rifle Bay

Did you know?

There is a secret tunnel system underneath the fort. Keep a weathered eye out for the stairs that lead down into this lesser known area of Tom Sawyer island.

Did you know?

As you walk the streets of Frontierland, notice the ground beneath your feet. Imprinted on the ground are images of horse shoes, boots, and wagon ruts, showing the residents of Frontierland moving around the town. This little detail brings the old west back to life as you walk along a dirt road.

Tomorrowland

As you enter Tomorrowland, be prepared to experience space flight, interstellar bad guys and some of your favorite super-heroes. Try your skills at Buzz Lightyear Space Ranger Spin or zoom through the stars on Space Mountain.

Buzz Lightyear's Space Ranger Spin

1. ★★ As you approach the Buzz Lightyear Space Ranger Spin attraction, you will see two batteries at the base of the attraction sign. What type of batteries are these?
   a. C
   b. AAA
   c. D
   d. 9 Volt

2. ★ As you enter the building take a moment to examine the map of space. Which sector is Planet Z located in?
   a. Sector 7
   b. Sector 5
   c. Sector 9
   d. Sector 6

3. ★ As you see the drawing of the space cruiser, what is the model number on the drawing?
   a. PX-37
   b. 37-XP
   c. 37-PX
   d. XP-37

4. ⭐⭐ As you begin your adventure, what does the read-out say on the Gigantobot?
   a. Buzz Rules
   b. Space Rules
   c. Zurg Rules
   d. Blaster Party

> ### Did you know?
> In the first room on the Buzz Lightyear Space Ranger Spin, try to hit the red robots left hand and get 100,000 points per hit.

5. ⭐ As you finish your time at the Buzz Lightyear Space Ranger Spin take a look at the score rankings. Which of the rankings is seen in yellow?
   a. Planetary Pilot
   b. Space Ace
   c. Space Cadet
   d. Galactic Hero

6. ⭐⭐ As you exit the Buzz Lightyear Space Ranger Spin attraction, read the label on the batteries. Which town are the batteries made in?
   a. Glendale
   b. Orlando
   c. Anaheim
   d. Marceline

---

7. ⭐⭐⭐ As you wander through Tomorrowland, stop at the Robo-Newz stand. Which Disney character picture is seen on the front page?
   a. Buzz Lightyear
   b. Dopey
   c. Stitch
   d. Snow White

8. ⭐ Stop by the Thirst Scanner for a cold drink. Finish the line on the sign, "Delivering refreshment to a thirsty _____."
   a. Space
   b. Galaxy
   c. Alien
   d. Astronaut

The Great Walt Disney World Scavenger Hunt

Walt Disney's Carousel of Progress

9. ★★ As you approach the Carousel of Progress, take a moment to read about this attraction on the sign. In which year did this attraction premier at the New York World's Fair?
    a. 1984-85
    b. 1954-55
    c. 1964-65
    d. 1971-72

Did you know?

If you look out the window in the scene from 1940, you will see a sign that reads "Herb Ryman Attorney at Law" This refers to Herb Ryman, a long-time animator for Walt Disney.

10. ★ Finish this line of the Carousel of Progress song. "There's a great big beautiful tomorrow, shining at the end of every _____."
    a. Year
    b. Week
    c. Night
    d. Day

11. ★ As your host greets you, what special day does he tell you this is?
    a. Valentine's day
    b. His birthday
    c. New Year's Day
    d. Halloween

12. ★★ As your host tells you about the new inventions, how long does it take you to travel from New York to Los Angeles?
    a. Less than 10 days
    b. Less than 7 days
    c. Less than a month
    d. Less than 3 days

13. ★★ With the new wash day marvel, how long does it take to do the laundry?
    a. 5 days
    b. 2 days
    c. 5 hours
    d. 2 hours

> ### Did you know?
> If you listen closely to uncle Orville, you may recognize his voice. This character was voiced by veteran voice over artist Mel Blanc. Blanc was known as the voice of Bugs Bunny, Yosemite Sam and Foghorn Leghorn as well as dozens of other animated characters during his long career.

14. ★★ Where is the World's Fair located according to your host?
    a. Los Angeles
    b. Orlando
    c. Marceline
    d. St. Louis

15. ★★ As you enter the 1920's, what does your host tell you that new jazz music is like?
    a. The bee's knees
    b. The dog's tuxedo
    c. The chicken's cackle
    d. The cat's meow

16. ★ What character is your host playing in the July 4th parade?
    a. Benjamin Franklin
    b. George Washington
    c. Abraham Lincoln
    d. Benedict Arnold

> ### Did you know?
> In every scene during the Carousel of Progress, you will notice your host accompanied by his faithful dog Rover.

17. ★ What character is the daughter playing for the 4th of July according to her costume?
    a. Statue of Liberty
    b. Martha Washington
    c. Susan B. Anthony
    d. Betsy Ross

18. ★★ In the third scene, we see our host sitting at the kitchen table. What color is the table cloth?

a.	White	c.	Yellow
b.	Blue	d.	Tan

19. ★ What new term did our host hear coined on the radio?
    - a. Mouse house
    - b. Rat race
    - c. Thing a ma bob
    - d. Do-hickey

20. ★ What type of program is the grandmother watching on the television?
    - a. Baseball
    - b. Soap Opera
    - c. Music
    - d. Boxing

21. ★★ What is your host's wife doing in the other room while he tells you about the 1940's?
    - a. Washing
    - b. Sewing
    - c. Wallpapering
    - d. Bathing

22. ★ What does the grandfather tell them he wants the refrigerator to bring him?
    - a. Root beer
    - b. Pepsi
    - c. Dr. Pepper
    - d. Sprite

23. ★★ As you look around the room, what type of Christmas decoration adorns the fireplace mantle?
    - a. Candles
    - b. Nutcrackers
    - c. Bells
    - d. Pictures

24. ★ How hot does the oven get before it overloads and burns the turkey?
    - a. 550
    - b. 1075
    - c. 975
    - d. 725

Did you know?

The hidden Mickey in this attraction is the nutcracker sitting atop the fireplace mantle in the fourth scene.

Catherine F. Olen

Monster's Inc. Laugh Floor

25. ★ As you are waiting for your time on the laugh floor, take a look at the vending machine on the left. What is the item in the lower left side called?
    a. Monkey bar
    b. Opossum bar
    c. Raccoon bar
    d. Gopher bar

26. ★★ As you read the forms on the notice board, what does number 4 read on the right column of the RSI form?
    a. Stretch your wings
    b. Clean horns make healthy horns
    c. Sing after you scream
    d. Stoop, Stand and Stretch

27. ★★ According to the notice on the board, what day of the week is the scream seminar?
    a. Tuesday
    b. Thursday
    c. Monday
    d. Saturday

28. ★ As you take your seat and the show begins, what does Roz say might happen if you don't generate enough screams?
    a. You're fired
    b. The doors won't open
    c. You will have to adopt a monster
    d. Boo will not get to see Sully

Did you know?

You can text your jokes to the monster's and, if selected, they will be read by the performers during your show on the laugh floor.

Tomorrowland Transit Authority PeopleMover

29. ★★ As you enter your vehicle for the Tomorrowland Transit Authority, your narrator calls it, "The highway in _____."
    a. Tomorrowland
    b. The future
    c. The sky
    d. The Magic Kingdom

30. ★ The People Mover is perfect for what kind of activity according to your narrator?
    a. Relaxing
    b. Taking a nap
    c. Figuring out what to ride next
    d. People watching

> **Did you know?**
>
> As you enter the first tunnel you will ride by a large model city. This is the original model made for Walt Disney for Epcot. Originally, Epcot was supposed to be a self-sustaining city of tomorrow. It was after his death that the imagineers changed the concept and the Epcot we know today was born.

31. ★★★ Read the poster for Pan-Galactic Pizza. The tag line reads, "Hot delivery, right to your_____."
    a. Planet
    b. Door
    c. Galaxy
    d. Solar system

32. ★★ What does the sign say just below the robot sitting in the monitoring booth?
    a. Watch your step
    b. Watch your rollers
    c. Out of order
    d. Tomorrowland, come back tomorrow

33. ✯ As you travel through Space Mountain look just above your head. What do you see upside down above you?
    a. Green aliens
    b. Robots
    c. Space pods
    d. Astronauts

> **Did you know?**
>
> As you travel through Space Mountain, you will see the roller coaster whizzing by you occasionally. If you are one of the lucky few to ride the Tomorrowland Transit Authority while this attraction is down, you may get a glimpse of Space Mountain with the lights on.

34. ✯✯ Listen carefully for the female voice paging Mr. Tom Morrow. Who does the voice tell him to see?
    a. Mr. Smith
    b. Mr. Jones
    c. Mr. Disney
    d. Mr. Johnson

35. ✯ As you narrator talks about The Carousel of Progress, in what century does this family take you back to?
    a. 18th
    b. 19th
    c. 20th
    d. 21st

36. ✯ Which character from Toy Story do you hear speaking to you as you enter the next attraction after the Carousel of Progress?
    a. Buzz Lightyear
    b. Emperor Zurg
    c. The aliens
    d. Woody

37. ✯✯ As you pass by the Monster's Inc. Laugh Floor. Which character from Monster's Inc. tells you to keep it moving?
    a. Mike Wazowski
    b. Roz
    c. Sully
    d. Randall Boggs

> ### Did you know?
> Disneyland resort in California had a people mover system in Tomorrowland but this was removed to make way for a new attraction. Now, if you visit Disneyland, you can see the track remains in this area of the park. For a better view of the track from this attraction, ride the monorail.

38. ★★ As you ride above Tomorrowland you will see a group of Little Green Men above one of the souvenir kiosks. How many do you see?
    a. 9
    b. 10
    c. 11
    d. 14

EPCOT

Introduction

Opening on October 1, 1982, Epcot is the brain child of founder Walt Disney. Experimental Prototype Community of Tomorrow, Disney wanted to create a living functioning community within Walt Disney World with residents living and interacting with the theme park guests. While this vision ultimately was scrapped with the death of Disney, the imagineers took the theme park in two distinctive directions. Technology and innovation in the front part of the park and a world showcase on the back part of Epcot. Let us take you through the exciting world of Epcot.

Future World East

Walk through the gates of Epcot and into a land where the future awaits you. Ride on Spaceship Earth to see how technology has evolved since the beginning of recorded history. Travel beneath the ocean with Nemo and his friends to see how our aquatic friends have evolved. Rocket to Mars on Mission Space or test your own state of the art vehicle on Test Track.

Spaceship Earth

1. ★★★ As you begin your journey on Spaceship Earth, listen carefully. What famous actress narrates your journey?
   a. Judi Dench
   b. Tina Fey
   c. Betty White
   d. Ellen DeGeneres

> **Did you know?**
> The entire structure of Spaceship Earth can fit into the aquarium tank in The Living Seas building at Epcot.

2. ★★ How many years pass between the struggle to survive and the first recorded cave wall images?

	a.	15 years		c.	15 hundred years
	b.	15 thousand years		d.	15 million years

3. ★★ As you enter ancient Egypt, what is the man pounding flat to make papyrus?
   - a. Seaweed
   - b. Water lilies
   - c. Reeds
   - d. Crab grass

> **Did you know?**
>
> The hieroglyphics on the wall behind the pharaoh are actual writings from ancient Egypt.

4. ★ Which civilization created the alphabet you know today?
   - a. Egyptians
   - b. Chinese
   - c. French
   - d. Phoenicians

> **Did you know?**
>
> The geodesic sphere formation of Spaceship Earth has grooves built in so the rain water runs into a drainage system that pumps the water into the fountain in the center of Epcot. This saves the guests from getting soaked as they walk beneath the Spaceship Earth attraction.

5. ★★ What did the Roman's build all over the world according to your narrator?
   - a. Walls
   - b. Roads
   - c. Libraries
   - d. Theme Parks

6. ★ In which city does the library that burns reside after Rome falls?
   - a. Alexandria
   - b. Constantinople
   - c. Istanbul
   - d. Amsterdam

The Great Walt Disney World Scavenger Hunt

7. ★★ Which inventor developed the moveable type printing press?
   a. Michelangelo
   b. Guttenberg
   c. Da Vinci
   d. Benjamin Franklin

> **Did you know?**
>
> As you ride through the renaissance era, you will look up and see Michelangelo painting the ceiling of the Sistine Chapel in Rome.

8. ★★ As you travel through the early part of the 20th century you will see a radio show. Which of these signs is *not* on the wall underneath the clocks?
   a. Local
   b. London
   c. New York
   d. Eastern

9. ★★ In a garage in which state does the next innovation in communication take place?
   a. New York
   b. North Carolina
   c. Michigan
   d. California

10. ★★ According to your narrator, how many years have shaped the world you live in today?
    a. 3,000
    b. 300,000
    c. 30,000
    d. 30,000,000

> **Did you know?**
>
> Take some time to answer the questions on the display screen in your ride vehicle to see how you will live in the future. This is a fun way to interact with the Spaceship Earth attraction.

Mission SPACE

11. ★★★ As you approach the Mission Space attraction, pause for a few moments to look around you. According to the plaques, which historic figure said these words, "Look upward…from this world to the heavens."
    a. Aristotle
    b. Plato
    c. Ulysses
    d. Da Vinci

12. ★★★ As you examine the large sphere outside this attraction on which date did the USSR Lunar 20 take place?
    a. August 14, 1969
    b. December 2, 1997
    c. February 14, 1972
    d. October 28, 1928

13. ★★★ Find the quote from Arthur C. Clark, Finish the quote, "The only way of discovering the limits of the possible is to venture a little way past them into the _____."
    a. Unknown
    b. Impossible
    c. Future
    d. Universe

> ### Did you know?
> You can request a green or orange boarding pass for this attraction, one will give you the full ride effect with the centrifuge while the green will give you a ride without the spin for a gentler experience.

14. ★★ As you enter the building and read the plaques on the walls, who was the first man in space?
    a. Neil Armstrong
    b. Yuri Gagarin
    c. Buzz Aldrin
    d. Valentina Tereshkova

15. ★★ On what date did the first untethered spacewalk occur?

a. February 7, 1984 c. February 20, 1964
b. July 15, 1975 d. September 1, 2030

> ### Did you know?
>
> If you look very carefully at the center of the space wheel, you will see a small logo for the Horizons attraction that was housed in this building prior to Mission Space being built in 2000.

16. ★★ As you look at the astronaut photos, what breed of dog appears with the first family in outer space?
    a. Husky   c. German Shepherd
    b. Chihuahua   d. Dalmatian

17. ★★ As you read the plaque for the first man on the moon, which of these is *not* one of the names listed?
    a. Buzz Aldrin   c. Sheldon Cooper
    b. Neil Armstrong   d. Michael Collins

18. ★ As you listen to the preflight video, what are you lacking that the space heroes had?
    a. Courage   c. A space craft
    b. Physical build d. Training

19. ★ As you listen to your narrator, what is the X-2 deep space shuttle powered by?
    a. Solid Oxygen   c. Solid Tritogen
    b. Solid Nitrogen d. Solid Hydrogen

20. ★★ Your X-2 deep space shuttle can accelerate from zero to what speed in sixty seconds?
    a. 600   c. 60,000
    b. 6,000 d. 600,000

21. ★★ Which of these is *not* one of the positions for your team?

a. Astronaut
c. Navigator
b. Commander
d. Engineer

22. ★ What planet are you and your team training for on the orange team?
    a. Pluto
    c. Neptune
    b. Mars
    d. Uranus

> **Did you know?**
>
> According to NASA, it would take somewhere between six and eight months to travel the distance to Mars. The longest time spent in space was fourteen months by Valeri Polyakov who lived on the Mir space station. This record was a total of four-hundred thirty-seven days.

23. ★ What is the job of the engineer on your training mission?
    a. Fire thrusters
    b. Deploy shields
    c. Activating manual controls for landing
    d. Activate hyper sleep

24. ★ What emergency comes up for your training crew that you must navigate around?
    a. Alien space craft
    c. Meteor storm
    b. Ran out of fuel
    d. Death star hits planet

Test Track

> **Did you know?**
>
> Test track is the fastest attraction at Walt Disney World with a top speed of sixty-five miles per hour on the outside portion of the track. This beats even roller coasters like Aerosmith's Rockin' Roller Coaster at Disney Studios.

Did you know?

As you walk through the queue for Test Track, take a look around at the photographs of the children. These are the actual children of Walt Disney World imagineers.

Did you know?

Test Track is built to withstand hurricane force winds, due to the weather issues in the central Florida area. Even with these reinforcements, Test Track will shut down when there is lightening in the immediate area.

Did you know?

As you begin your power test, the doors in front of you open automatically. The original attraction used this area for crash testing. The car catapulting towards the wall while accelerating towards the barrier. The doors opened at the last second to reveal the outside track.

Future World West

The Land

25. ★★ As you enter the building for The Land, you will notice quotes on the walls on the lower level neat the queue for Living with the Land. Name the author of the quote, "It is important to save the earth because that's all we have. We don't get another."
    a. Pope John Paul II
    b. Amy Larrick
    c. Rousseau
    d. Kim Phelan

26. ★★ Reading the quotes on the walls, finish this line by Kathy Hemeon's sixth grade class, "Our environment is like a _____."
    a. Colorful mosaic
    b. Beautiful garden
    c. Gleaming sunsphere
    d. Patchwork quilt

27. ★★ Finish this quote by Robert G. Ingersol, "In nature there are neither rewards nor _____, there are consequences."
    a. Punishments
    b. Payments
    c. Practices
    d. Sufferings

The Great Walt Disney World Scavenger Hunt

Living with the Land

28. ★★ As your ride vehicle approaches, take a moment to look at the mural adorning the wall behind the loading area. What farm equipment does the farmer hold in his hands?
    a. Hoe
    b. Rake
    c. Scythe
    d. Flail

29. ★ As you ride through the rain forest, what animal do you see staring at you from the shore to your left?
    a. Alligator
    b. Turtle
    c. Monkey
    d. Snake

30. ★ As you enter the growing area, your narrator refers to this area as the _____ laboratory.
    a. Growing
    b. Plant
    c. Agriculture
    d. Living

31. ★ According to your narrator, what region is home to the great diversity of plants on the planet?
    a. The desert
    b. The tropics
    c. The rain forest
    d. The ocean

32. ★★ The dragon fruit is a member of what family of plants?
    a. Agave
    b. Grape
    c. Cacao
    d. Cactus

33. ★ What is the most popular fruit in the world according to your narrator?
    a. Bananas
    b. Tomato
    c. Grapes
    d. Apples

34. ★★ Fish farming accounts for how much of the fish we eat annually?
    a. One quarter
    b. One third
    c. One half
    d. Three quarters

35. ★ How many head of lettuce are grown in the small area you see on your tour according to your narrator?
    a. 27,000
    b. 37,000
    c. 47,000
    d. 22,000

36. ★★ Which of these is *not* one of the groups your narrator lists as people doing their part to help with growing our agriculture needs?
    a. Scientists
    b. Fishermen
    c. Back yard gardeners
    d. Farmers

Soarin' Around the World

37. ★★★ Which famous actor gives your security checklist prior to your flight?
    a. Patrick Warburton
    b. Kurt Russell
    c. David Spade
    d. Josh Gad

38. ★ As you are told to use the storage under your seat, what is the guest in the video wearing on his head?
    a. Goofy Ears
    b. Sorcerer Hat
    c. Mickey Ears
    d. Princess Hat

> ### Did you know?
> As you watch the pre-flight video, notice the couple at the end of the row are wearing flight jackets and goggles on their heads.

> ### Did you know?
> The monument for the Taj Mahal was digitally rendered as the actual monument is a no-fly zone due to terrorist concerns.

39. ★ What does your flight attendant refer to children as in the video?
    a. Little people
    b. Children
    c. Munchkins
    d. Little aviators

40. ★★★ As you begin your journey on Soarin', you will see a mountain looming, which mountain is depicted in this first clip?
    a. Kilimanjaro
    b. Mount Blanc
    c. Matterhorn
    d. Mount Fuji

41. ★★ As you soar over the polar ice caps, what type of whale do you see?
    a. Blue whale
    b. Killer whale
    c. Humpback whale
    d. Beluga whale

42. ★★★ As you soar over the German countryside, you will see an iconic castle, what is the name of this castle?
    a. Buckingham Palace
    b. Neuschwanstein Castle
    c. Balnagown Castle
    d. Versailles

Did you know?

The Neuschwanstein castle was used as inspiration for Sleeping Beauty Castle at Disneyland resort.

43. ★ As you soar over the African savanna, what kind of animal is featured in this clip?
    a. Zebra
    b. Lion
    c. Cheetah
    d. Elephant

44. ★ As you soar over the Great Wall of China, what activity are the people enjoying?
    a. Kite flying
    b. Jogging
    c. Tai Chi
    d. Hula Hooping

45. ★★★ As you soar over the Taj Mahal in India, what is the purpose of this structure?
    a. Mausoleum
    b. Castle
    c. Theme park
    d. War memorial

46. ★★ As you soar over an enormous waterfall, what is the name of this landmark?
    a. Niagara Falls
    b. Angel Falls
    c. Victoria Falls
    d. Iguazu Falls

47. ★★ In what city does the Eiffel Tower stand?
    a. London
    b. Paris
    c. New York
    d. Anaheim

48. ★ As you arrive at Walt Disney World just in time for fireworks, which theme park are you soaring over?
    a. Magic Kingdom
    b. Animal Kingdom
    c. Epcot
    d. Disney Studios

> ### Did you know?
> This attraction was originally brought to Walt Disney World as part of the Disneyland 50th anniversary. The original Soarin' Over California gave visitors to Epcot the opportunity to see one of the attractions from Disney's California Adventure.

The Seas with Nemo and Friends

The Seas with Nemo and Friends attraction

49. ★ As you enter the building and begin your walk through the beach, what is the name of this beach?
    a. Coral Reef
    b. Coral Shell
    c. Coral Caves
    d. Coral Sands

50. ★ Stop for a moment to read the grouping of signs. What sort of bird is there a preserve sign for?
    a. Pelican
    b. Seagull
    c. Owl
    d. Water Fowl

Did you know?

On the sign for Sharks Sighted, notice the silhouettes of Bruce, Anchor and Chum from *Finding Nemo*. The three sharks who hold a meeting to stop eating fish. "Fish are friends, not food."

51. ★ If you look at the surf conditions sign on the lifeguard tower, what does the sign arrow point to?
    a. Mild
    b. Just Swell
    c. Dangerous
    d. Choppy

52. ★★ As you enter your shell and begin your journey with Nemo and his friends, what is the name of his school teacher that sings to his students?
    a. Mr. Fish
    b. Mr. Ray
    c. Mr. Stingray
    d. Mr. Manta

53. ★★ As you see Marlin and Dory, what name does she call out looking for Nemo?
    a. Bingo
    b. Chico
    c. Fabio
    d. Groucho

54. ★ When you hear Squirt and Nemo, what does Squirt tell Nemo to grab?
    a. Turtle
    b. Kelp
    c. Shell
    d. Bubbles

55. ★★ What is the name of Nemo's starfish friend you see stuck to the glass as you ride by?
    a. Pinky
    b. Peach
    c. Cuddle
    d. Flo

Did you know?

If you look beyond the animation to the fish, you are seeing the actual fish in the aquarium. The imagineers at Walt Disney World incorporated the attraction ride into the aquarium to give guests an immersive experience.

The Great Walt Disney World Scavenger Hunt

SeaBase

56. ★★ As you enter the aquarium area, find the sharks. As you read the warning signs in the BITE YOU area, which of these completes this warning, "If you see a _____, it does NOT mean it is safe to swim."
    a. Dolphin
    b. Whale
    c. Fish
    d. Shark

57. ★★ As you read about safety, finish this sign, "Don't wear _____ colored clothing."
    a. Any
    b. Blue
    c. Black
    d. Bright

58. ★★ As you continue your discovery of the aquarium area, how many million undiscovered marine lives are there in the world?
    a. 8 million
    b. 80 million
    c. 800 million
    d. 8 thousand

59. ★★ Continue your exploration of the signs around the aquarium area. What substance are coral reefs made up of?
    a. Calcium chloride
    b. Calcium carbonate
    c. Calcium Hydrogen
    d. Calcium phosphate

60. ★★ How does the Moray eel breathe according to the sign outside the eel tank?
    a. Flapping its gills
    b. Going to the surface
    c. Snapping its jaws
    d. Kissing other fish

Catherine F. Olen

> ### Did you know?
> You can schedule special tours within this pavilion to swim with the dolphins, swim in the coral reef or scuba dive in the tank with the cast members. While the aquarium area itself is impressive, these specialized tours give guests up close and personal time with the sea life.

61. ★ As you continue your exploration of the aquariums, stop for a moment to read the sign about the dolphins. What sort of animal are dolphins?
    a. Aquatic
    b. Reptiles
    c. Mammals
    d. Insect

62. ★★ As you pause to read the sign about sharks, what are their skeletons made from?
    a. Cartilage
    b. Bone
    c. Rubber
    d. Tendon

63. ★ Which sea animal is known as the pop stars of the deep?
    a. Dolphin
    b. Angel fish
    c. Manatee
    d. Humpback whale

> ### Did you know?
> Take some time to join Crush at Turtle Talk, a completely interactive show with Crush the turtle chatting with the little explorers. This new technology allows the animated character to chat in real time with the audience so no two shows are ever the same.

Imagination!

Journey into Imagination with Figment

64. ★ As you enter the queue for Journey into Imagination with Figment, what is Dr. Wayne Szalinski known for according to his picture?
    a. Microscope
    b. Shrink ray
    c. Singing sword
    d. Talking turtles

Did you know?

As you experience this attraction, take a moment to notice the reference to Medfield college. This college was the name used for many of the early Disney films including, *The Computer Wore Tennis Shoes, The Absent-Minded Professor* and *Son of Flubber.*

65. ★ As you pass by the door for Dr. Nigel Channing's office, which of these is *not* one of his jobs?
    a. Director of Operations
    b. Manager of Everything Else
    c. Head of Laboratories
    d. Custodian

66. ★★ As we begin our journey and first see Figment the dragon, what is he holding in his hands?
    a. A microscope
    b. A bicycle
    c. A trumpet
    d. A suitcase

67. ★ As figment lists the five senses what does he say Dr. Channing tastes like?
    a. Chicken
    b. Apple
    c. Flubber
    d. Orange

68. ★ As we enter the sound lab and Figment appears, what color is the telephone he holds in his hand?
    a. Blue
    b. Purple
    c. Red
    d. Yellow

69. ★★ As you enter the sight room, what does the third line on the eye chart read?
    a. F I G
    b. I O Z
    c. D I S
    d. W E D

70. ★ In the smell lab, what scent does Figment spray at you?
    a. Smelly garbage
    b. Wet dog
    c. Skunk
    d. Rotten apple

71. ★ As you pass by the office door to the next room, what sort of testing is going on in this room?
    a. Tickle testing
    b. Sleep testing
    c. Puzzle testing
    d. SAT testing

72. ★ As we see the finale of Journey into Imagination with Figment, what everyday item is used as a hot air balloon?
    a. Tear drop
    b. Mickey Balloon
    c. Cotton candy
    d. Light blub

Did you know?

Guests can enter the Disney Pixar Theater and watch several short films in 3D. Stop in to see your favorite Pixar short films.

World Showcase

Travel through the countries of the world as you walk through the World Showcase. Sample exotic cuisine and walk through the streets of France, Italy, Germany, China, Japan, Mexico, Norway, Canada and the United States of America all in one day.

Be sure to stop and watch performers demonstrate their talents in authentic costumes and pick up international souvenirs during your time in the World Showcase.

> **Did you know?**
>
> The cast members working within the pavilions of the World Showcase are all natives of the countries they represent.

Canada

1. ★★ As you approach the northwest mercantile, in what year was this established according to the sign you see on the outside of the shop?
    a. 1790
    b. 1970
    c. 1977
    d. 1955

The Great Walt Disney World Scavenger Hunt

> **Did you know?**
>
> Of the three totem poles that stand in this pavilion, only one was carved out of wood, the other two are fiber glass.

2. ★★ As you enter the Northwest Mercantile, take a look at the four canisters on the shelf high above your head. What is the maker of the coffee?
   a. Fluffy
   b. Columbian
   c. Sunshine
   d. Disney

3. ★★ If you read the sign on how to make maple syrup, how many gallons of sap produce one gallon on syrup?
   a. 4 gallons
   b. 400 gallons
   c. 40 gallons
   d. 1 gallon

O' Canada

4. ★ As you enter the theater for O' Canada, what famous comedian is your host for this feature film?
   a. Steve Martin
   b. George Carlin
   c. Martin Short
   d. Chevy Chase

5. ★ As you travel over Niagara Falls, what is this part of the falls named?
   a. Wet falls
   b. Maple Leaf Falls
   c. Mountie Falls
   d. Horseshoe Falls

6. ★ As you travel to New Brunswick, how high does the tide get at high tide?
   a. Twenty feet
   b. Thirty feet
   c. Forty feet
   d. Fifty feet

7. ★ According to your host, what is a giveaway that it snows in Canada?
   a. Brown bears
   b. Polar bears
   c. Grizzly bears
   d. Teddy bears

8. ★ What does Martin Short say is the dream of every young Canadian?
   a. Pro hockey player
   b. Comedian
   c. Olympic curler
   d. Mountie

9. ★ According to your host, Calgary British Columbia is the gateway to what area?
   a. The Rocky Mountains
   b. The Pacific Ocean
   c. The United States
   d. The Forest Primeval

10. ★★ In what year was the Calgary Stampede established?
    a. 1914
    b. 1955
    c. 1912
    d. 2012

11. ★ Which is the only walled city in Canada?
    a. Calgary
    b. Banff
    c. Victoria
    d. Quebec

12. ★★ As you see the pictures of the stars that were born in Canada, which of these is *not* one you see listed?
    a. Leslie Nielsen
    b. Tom Hanks
    c. Keanu Reeves
    d. William Shatner

13. ★ As your tour of Canada comes to an end, which attractions does Martin tell you he has a FastPass for?
    a. Test track
    b. Mission Space
    c. Soarin'
    d. Frozen

The Great Walt Disney World Scavenger Hunt

United Kingdom

> ### Did you know?
> You can meet Alice, The Mad Hatter and other characters from Alice in Wonderland. Also, Winnie the Pooh, Tigger, Piglet and all the gang from your favorite Winnie the Pooh books and films. Check the Walt Disney World character time table for meet and greet times.

14. ★★ As you enter the United Kingdom pavilion, take a look at the large red mail box, what day, other than Christmas, is there no mail collection?
    a. Boxing day
    b. Easter
    c. Fourth of July
    d. Thanksgiving

15. ★★ Step into the Crown and Crest shop and stop for a moment to look at the wooden dolls in the display. What is the animal sitting on the tray in front of the king in this scene?
    a. Goose
    b. Pig
    c. Cow
    d. Elk

16. ★ How many trumpeters do you see above the royal court, in this scene?
    a. 3
    b. 4
    c. 6
    d. 5

17. ★★ If you look high above you will find a glass case with four human items, what are these items?
    a. Eyes
    b. Hands
    c. Feet
    d. Skulls

> **Did you know?**
>
> If you look at the chimneys of the buildings around the United Kingdom pavilion, you will see soot. This is to make this area more authentic to the United Kingdom, as the residents have been using their fire places to keep warm.

18. ★★ As you step into the garden areas, look for a box with the life cycle of the butterfly. Which of these is *not* one of the stages of this cycle?
    a. Egg
    b. Pupa
    c. Adult
    d. Hatching

> **Did you know?**
>
> If you look up at the windows above The Queen's Table, you will see four stained glass windows. The crests displayed are the four major colleges in United Kingdom. Oxford, Cambridge, Edinburgh and Eton.

France

> **Did you know?**
>
> You can meet Aurora from Sleeping Beauty or Belle from Beauty and the Beast during your time in France. Check the Walt Disney World character time table for meet and greet times.

19. ★★ As you cross the bridge to the France pavilion take a moment to admire the Eiffel Tower above the shops. How tall is this scale monument to France?
    a. 986 feet
    b. 103 feet
    c. 986 inches
    d. 103 inches

The Great Walt Disney World Scavenger Hunt

Did you know?

Stop and enjoy the attraction Impressions de France, a feature film about the wonders of France. This is a wonderful way to discover more about this beautiful land.

Morocco

Did you know?

You can meet Aladdin and Jasmine from the classic film *Aladdin* during your stay in the Morocco pavilion. Check the Walt Disney World character time table for meet and greet times.

20. ★★ As you wander the narrow streets of the Morocco pavilion, find the sign for the Chellah Minaret. In what century was it reconstructed?
    a. 14th
    b. 15th
    c. 17th
    d. 21st

21. ★★ Continue your exploration of Morocco and find the Fez House. What was the traditional Moroccan house built around according to the plaque?
    a. Garden
    b. Swimming pool
    c. Courtyard
    d. Tennis court

22. ★★ Find the plaque for the Bab BoujouLoud. In what year was the main gate of the ancient city of Fez established?
    a. 920
    b. 1920
    c. 1786
    d. 786

23. ★★ What is the name of a specialize market where artisans create and display their wares in Morocco?
    a. Store
    b. Souk
    c. Plaza
    d. Piazza

24. ★★ Find the Kingdom of Morocco display within the buildings. What substance is used by Moroccan women to enhance their beauty?
    a. Mascara
    b. Coal
    c. Grease
    d. Kohl

25. ★★ In what ceremony does Henna take an important role?
    a. Birthday
    b. Funeral
    c. Wedding
    d. Coronation

26. ★★ Many Moroccan festivals are accompanied by what sort of equestrian extravaganza?
    a. Fantasia
    b. Gala
    c. Triumph
    d. Capriccio

Japan

27. ★ As you enter the Japan pavilion, walk towards the water. As you stand before the Torii, whom do the roosters welcome according to the plaque?
    a. The moon goddess
    b. The sun goddess
    c. The spring goddess
    d. The star goddess

28. ★★ As you stand before the five-story pagoda, which of these is not one of the elements Buddhists believe all things in the universe are produced from?
    a. Sky
    b. Earth
    c. Electricity
    d. Water

The Great Walt Disney World Scavenger Hunt

The American Adventure

> **Did you know?**
>
> Disney has a program called the Heroes Work Here program. Walt Disney World hires our nations veterans, trains them and supports them when they return to our country from their duty around the globe.

29. ★ Enter the building for The American Adventure and find the painting with the large airplane. What is the name of this painting?
    a. Defending America
    b. Defending freedom
    c. Defending the skies
    d. The Wright Brothers first flight

30. ★★ As you read the famous quotes on the walls, finish this famous quote by Jane Adams, "What after all has maintained the human race on this old _____ despite all the calamities of nature and all the tragic failings of mankind, if not faith in new possibilities and courage to advocate them."
    a. Globe
    b. World
    c. Earth
    d. Country

> **Did you know?**
>
> The paintings you see around the rooms of The American Adventure building are all done by Walt Disney Imagineers. Stop and admire the great artistic abilities of these highly talented individuals.

31. ★★ Walt Elias Disney made this famous quote, finish the line, "Our greatest natural resource is the minds of our _____."

a. Artists c. Scientists
b. Inventors d. Children

32. ✯✯ What is the title of the painting of the astronauts and the space shuttle?
    a. Reaching for the heavens
    b. Blasting Off
    c. Reaching for the stars
    d. The history of space flight

33. ✯✯✯ As you enter the museum and begin your exploration, in what year did the Mayflower arrive in Massachusetts?
    a. 1620 c. 1624
    b. 1619 d. 1688

34. ✯✯✯ At what age did Benjamin Banneker begin his study of astronomy?
    a. Fifty-eight c. Fifty-nine
    b. Sixty d. Seventy-seven

35. ✯✯ In what year was the statue of liberty dedicated in New York?
    a. 1886 c. 1881
    b. 1882 d. 1977

36. ✯✯ In 1917 the 89th regiment is sent to fight in France. What was the name of this regiment?
    a. Harlem Globetrotters
    b. Harlem resistance
    c. Harlem hell fighters
    d. Harlem regiment

The American Adventure

37. ✯✯ What famous author cohosts The American Experience with Benjamin Franklin?
    a. John Steinbeck c. Dan Brown
    b. Thomas Paine d. Mark Twain

The Great Walt Disney World Scavenger Hunt

38. ★ What is one of our national passions according to Benjamin Franklin?
    a. Humility
    b. Pride
    c. Nationalism
    d. Baseball

39. ★★ What do the people who came to the new world to find freedom call themselves according to the song you hear?
    a. Settlers
    b. Europeans
    c. Pilgrims
    d. Indians

40. ★★ Which monarch were the colonials fighting against during the Boston tea party?
    a. King George III
    b. King Henry VIII
    c. King Kong
    d. King Arthur

41. ★ As Benjamin Franklin talks with Thomas Jefferson, what famous document is he writing?
    a. The Constitution
    b. The Bill of Rights
    c. The Declaration of Independence
    d. The Magna Carta

42. ★★ As we hear Mr. Jefferson speak about the drafts, he says, "One stroke of this pen brings _____ from Congress?
    a. Forty changes
    b. Four changes
    c. Three changes
    d. Two changes

43. ★★ As Thomas Jefferson begins reading from The Declaration of Independence, he states that all men are endowed by whom with inalienable rights?
    a. Their president
    b. Their creator
    c. Their government
    d. Their parents

44. ★★ Which of these is *not* one of the rights listed in the Declaration of Independence?
    a. Liberty
    b. The pursuit of happiness
    c. Money
    d. Life

45. ★★ As you listen to the song about the revolutionary war, what do the colony soldiers call the British soldiers?
    a. Lobster backs
    b. Crab backs
    c. Lobster Thermidor
    d. Octopus backs

46. ★★ As you hear Fredrick Douglas speak, he references what famous book?
    a. *Gone with the Wind*
    b. *Uncle Tom's Cabin*
    c. *Huckleberry Finn*
    d. *The Underground Railroad*

47. ★★ What famous war is referenced in the song about two brothers going to war?
    a. World War I
    b. World War II
    c. The Civil War
    d. The Revolutionary War

48. ★ In what city was the exhibition of 1876 held?
    a. Washington D.C.
    b. Philadelphia
    c. New York
    d. St. Louis

49. ★ What famous woman is speaking when you see the exhibition of 1876?
    a. Harriet Beecher Stowe
    b. Betsy Ross
    c. Susan B. Anthony
    d. Martha Washington

50. ★ As we see the inventions flickering across the screen, which leaves its frame first?
    a. Airplane
    b. Movie projector
    c. Steam train
    d. Cable car

The Great Walt Disney World Scavenger Hunt

51. ★★ When you hear Teddy Roosevelt refer to the war to end all wars, which war was he speaking of?
    a. World War II
    b. The Civil War
    c. The Revolutionary War
    d. World War I

52. ★★ Charles Lindbergh flew across the Atlantic Ocean landing in Paris. What was the name of his plane?
    a. The Titanic
    b. The Spirit of St. Louis
    c. The Lusitania
    d. Queen of the Air

53. ★★ Which president uttered the famous words, "The only thing we have to fear, is fear itself."
    a. Franklin D. Roosevelt
    b. Teddy Roosevelt
    c. George Washington
    d. Ronald Reagan

54. ★★ What happened to our country on December 7, 1941, a day that will live in infamy?
    a. World Trade Center attack
    b. Lindbergh baby kidnapped
    c. Pearl Harbor attack
    d. The Civil War ends

55. ★★ As you sit back and listen to the song about America, watch the images on the screen. Which Disney character appears with Walt Disney?
    a. Tinker Bell
    b. Mickey Mouse
    c. Oswald the Lucky Rabbit
    d. Goofy

56. ★★ At the end of the song about America, what famous landmark do you see Mark Twain and Benjamin Franklin standing on?
    a. The Empire State Building
    b. Congress
    c. The White House
    d. The Statue of Liberty

Italy

> ### Did you know?
> If you walk down towards the lake, notice the striped poles in the water, this area is reminiscent of Venice with its gondolas and water ways.

> ### Did you know?
> The bell tower is an exact replica of the tower in St. Mark Square in Venice. The top is layered in gold leaf.

Germany

> ### Did you know?
> Meet Pinocchio and Geppetto from your favorite film *Pinocchio* during your visit to Germany. Check Walt Disney World meet and greet times.

> ### Did you know?
> The fountain in the center of this pavilion is topped with St. George slaying the dragon. In Germany myth, St. George saves the princess from her captivity by the dragon. These characters are symbolic of Germany saving Sweden from the invading armies.

The Great Walt Disney World Scavenger Hunt

China

> **Did you know?**
>
> Meet Mulan in the China pavilion. Check the Walt Disney World sites for times.

> **Did you know?**
>
> If you stand in the very center of the Temple of Heaven dome and speak, you hear a perfect amplification of your voice even if you whisper. Notice the four pillars in the center of the room representing the four seasons. The twelve pillars supporting the outer wall represent the twelve months of the Chinese calendar.

57. ★★ As you enter the China pavilion, what is the name of the large gate you pass through?
    a. Great Ming Gate
    b. Gate of the Golden Sun
    c. The Great Gate of China
    d. Gate of the Bronze Age

58. ★ As you wander through the China pavilion, find the replica of the army. What is the name of these warriors?
    a. Adobe Warrior
    b. Ceramic Warriors
    c. Terracotta Warriors
    d. Bronze Warriors

Reflections of China

59. ★★ How far did the Great Wall of China stretch at one time?
    a. Four-thousand miles
    b. Four hundred miles
    c. Four miles
    d. Forty-thousand miles

60. ★★ What profession does your host have?
    a. Historian
    b. Painter
    c. Poet
    d. Warrior

61. ★ Even in the hectic pace of modern China, there is always time for what according to your host?
    a. Jell-O
    b. Meditation
    c. Reflection
    d. Tai Chi

62. ★★ In China, they say, "A _____ in every painting."
    a. Piece of art
    b. Poem
    c. Moment
    d. Timeline

63. ★★ In the Gobi Desert, one still finds fellow travelers on what road?
    a. Desert
    b. China
    c. Lost City
    d. Silk

64. ★★ How long can the winter last in Heilongjiang?
    a. Six months
    b. Six weeks
    c. Six days
    d. Nine months

65. ★ What do the people of Heilongjiang do to celebrate the winter?
    a. Carve ice sculptures
    b. Make snow men
    c. Erect igloos
    d. Stay indoors

66. ★★ One of the treasures of china is the "nine _____ screen."
    a. Warriors
    b. Dragons
    c. Rivers
    d. Cherry Blossoms

67. ★★ The Forbidden City was home to how many emperor's?
    a. Thirteen
    b. Fifteen
    c. Twenty-four
    d. Ten

68. ★ The true face of China can be found where?
    a. The Forbidden City
    b. Hong Kong
    c. The mountains
    d. The faces of its people

Norway

69. ★★ As you come to the Norway Pavilion, notice the church. What century does this church reflect?
    a. 13th
    b. 14th
    c. 21st
    d. 18th

70. ★★ Look around the church at the ornate carvings, if you examine these carvings closely, which of the following were the creators?
    a. Huns
    b. Christians
    c. Norwegians
    d. Vikings

71. ★★★ As you wander the area around the church you will find a bronze statue. What does the statue of Grete Waitz commemorate?
    a. Sprinter
    b. 100-yard dash
    c. Jogging
    d. Marathon runner

72. ★★ As you explore the shops in the Norway pavilion, you will find a large figure to pose with for pictures. What kind of creature is this?
    a. Ogre
    b. Troll
    c. Cyclops
    d. Minotaur

Frozen Ever After

73. ★ As you enter the queue for Frozen Ever After, stop for a moment to look at the notices on the wall. What kind of sale on swimwear can you find at Oaken's Tokens?
    a. 10%
    b. 25 %
    c. 50%
    d. 100%

74. ★ Which person has been banned from Arendelle according to the notice on the wall?
    a. Duke of Weselton
    b. Hans of the Southern Isles
    c. Elsa
    d. Kristoff

75. ★ As you read the royal proclamation, what celebration are you invited to?
    a. Winter Snow Day Celebration
    b. Summer Snow Day Celebration
    c. Winter Solstice Celebration
    d. Princess Anna Birthday

Did you know?

As you enter Oaken's Token's keep an eye on the window of the sauna. You will see characters drawing on the foggy window and peeking at you from time to time.

76. ★★ As you enter your boat, which character from the movie *Frozen* gives your safety speech?
    a. Olaf
    b. Elsa
    c. Anna
    d. Oaken

77. ★★ As you see Olaf greeting you, which character is with him?
    a. Kristoff
    b. Anna
    c. Marshmallow
    d. Sven

78. ★ How many little rock trolls do you see around Grandfather Pabbie when he tells the story of Anna and Elsa?
    a. Four
    b. Ten
    c. Three
    d. Seven

79. ★ What activity is Olaf having fun with when you enter the ice palace?
    a. Ice skating
    b. Building a snowman
    c. Sledding
    d. Eating a snow cone

80. ★★ As you exit the palace, you will find which character surrounded by the little snowmen?
    a. Olaf
    b. Marshmallow
    c. Sven
    d. The Duke of Weselton

81. ★★★ One final thing before your time in Norway is complete. Find a large stone tablet with writing on it. What is this stone tablet called?
    a. Blarney stone
    b. Headstone
    c. Rune stone
    d. Gemstone

Did you know?

Throughout the day, you will find residents of Norway walking through this pavilion. Be sure to stop and get pictures with them before continuing your travels in the World Showcase.

Mexico

Did you know?

You can meet Donald Duck and his feathered friends from *The Three Caballeros* during your time in the Mexico pavilion. Check the Walt Disney World app for times.

82. ★★ As you enter the large pyramid, stop and look at the Mesoamerican timeline. Which civilization thrived between 900 – 1200 A.D.?
    a. Toltec
    b. Maya
    c. Olmec
    d. Aztec

83. ★★ In what year was the map of Cortez completed?
    a. 1452
    b. 1245
    c. 1425
    d. 1524

84. ★★ In the center of this room you will find a large round stone tablet with ancient markings. What was the use of this tablet to the culture?
    a. Calendar
    b. Musical instrument
    c. Fortune tellers stone
    d. Family tree

Grand Fiesta Tour starring the Three Caballeros

85. ★★ Which of these characters is *not* one of the Three Caballeros?
    a. Donald Duck
    b. Panchito
    c. Burrito
    d. Jose

86. ★★ As you begin your journey, what natural phenomenon appears behind the great pyramid to your left?
    a. Glacier
    b. Volcano
    c. Earthquake
    d. Tidal wave

87. ★ What sort of transportation do the Caballeros use to show you the wonders of Mexico?
    a. Hot air balloon
    b. Street car
    c. Burro
    d. Flying Serape

> **Did you know?**
>
> The skeleton figures on the bridge above your boat are representative of the Día De Los Muertos festival celebrating the loved ones that have passed on.

88. ★ As the children are hitting the piñata, which Disney character is depicted?
    a. Mickey Mouse
    b. Goofy
    c. Pluto
    d. Donald Duck

89. ★★ As you read the sky writing, what does "Donde Esta Donald?" mean in English?
    a. Where is Donald?
    b. We found Donald
    c. How is Donald?
    d. Do you love Donald?

90. ★ As Donald tries his hand a cliff diving, what color is his swim suit?
    a. Blue
    b. Yellow
    c. Red
    d. Green

91. ★ As you enter the fiesta, what instrument is Donald playing when you pass by him?
    a. Guitar
    b. Drum
    c. Violin
    d. Maracas

Disney Hollywood Studios

Introduction

Opening in 1989, Disney's Hollywood Studio is a trip to tinsel town. Walk down Hollywood Blvd. and eat at the famous Brown Derby restaurant. Watch Indiana Jones battle the forces of evil and join in the fun on the set of this classic film franchise and top off your time on Hollywood Blvd with a meet and greet with your favorite Disney characters.

Ride the freeways of L.A. with Aerosmith on Rockin' Roller Coaster and be taken to a different dimension on Tower of Terror. Party with your favorite Pixar friends in Toy Story Land, ride the Toy Story Midway Mania with Buzz and Woody.

Top your day at Disney Hollywood Studios with Star Wars shows, The Littler Mermaid, Frozen Ever After and Disney Junior.

Hollywood Blvd

Welcome to the heart of Hollywood. Look closely as you might see your favorite stars walking down this famous street. Be sure to take time out of your busy schedule to interact with the citizens of Hollywood as they go about their day.

Oscar's Super Service

1. ★★ Walk over to Oscar's Super Service and find the service attendant standing with a bottle of soda pop in his hand. What is the name of this service attendant?
   a. Tom
   b. Bo
   c. Jo
   d. Walt

2. ★ As you look over the tow truck for Oscar's, what is the phone number to call for service?
   a. Klondike 52099
   b. 407-939-5277
   c. KLondike 5320
   d. 714-781-4565

3. ★★ Oscar's Super Service advertises NeverNox with what special ingredient?
   a. Ethyl
   b. Petroleum
   c. Methane
   d. Hydrocarbon

4. ★★★ Look closely at the equipment at Oscar's Service Station, what city is the tire gauge manufactured in?
   a. Anaheim, California
   b. Orlando, Florida
   c. Tuscaloosa, Alabama
   d. Muskegon, Michigan

5. ★★ As you look inside the garage of Oscar's Super Service, find the blue and yellow can of motor oil. What brand of motor oil is on the label?
   a. Tomahawk
   b. Mohawk
   c. Kittyhawk
   d. Pennzoil

6. ★★ As you look at the gas pumps, how much does Oscar's charge for a gallon of gasoline?
   a. $1.99 9/10
   b. $.99 9/10
   c. $1.29 9/10
   d. $.19 9/10

---

7. ★★★ High above Hollywood Blvd you will find the billboard for Chevrolet. What is the license plate number of the truck you see in this billboard?
   a. B45RF
   b. S5RTY
   c. JSW4B
   d. TSB4W

8. ★ As you stand on Hollywood Blvd, find the billboard for the Red Car. What is the number of the red car pictured on this sign?
   a. 714
   b. 517
   c. 715
   d. 1977

Did you know?

As you walk down Hollywood Blvd, keep an eye out for the citizens of Hollywood. Chat with them and take photos as they greet visitors to their home town.

The Great Walt Disney World Scavenger Hunt

9. ★ Near the Antiques and Curios store you will find a brightly colored sign post. How many miles does it take to get to Tokyo according to the sign?
    a. 5626
    b. 2656
    c. 2532
    d. 1123

10. ★ As you read the signpost, which of these is *not* one of the cities on this sign?
    a. Rome
    b. Paris
    c. Anaheim
    d. Boston

11. ★ As you work your way down Hollywood Blvd, stop for a moment at Cover Story. Finish the tag line on the sign, "A star is _____."
    a. Made
    b. Born
    c. Here
    d. Discovered

12. ★★ Find the window with the advertisement that reads Melrose. What business is advertised on this window?
    a. Director
    b. Agent
    c. Lawyer
    d. Producer

13. ★★ As you read the billboards atop the buildings, which Donald Duck cartoon is being advertised?
    a. *Donald's Day Off*
    b. *Mr. Duck Steps Out*
    c. *Drippy Dippy Donald*
    d. *Autograph Hound*

14. ★ Just below the Donald Duck billboard, you will see the sign for Pluto's. Which of these is the correct sign outside Pluto's?
    a. Pluto's Toy Palace
    b. Pluto's Hot Dogs
    c. Pluto's Dog and Cat Emporium
    d. Pluto's Wonderful World of Cloth

> ### Did you know?
> Find the Darkroom along Hollywood Blvd. You will find the billboard for Hollywoodland property. When Hollywood was originally founded it was named for a housing development that was never realized.
>
> The sign remained and fell into disrepair with the LAND portion of the sign falling away. The residents of Hollywood paid to repair this iconic sign and it still remains to this day above the community of Hollywood in Southern California.

Celebrity 5 & 10

15. ★★★ As you enter the Celebrity 5 & 10 store, notice the celebrity photographs lining the walls. Behind the cash register counter find the photo 4th over from the left. Who is this famous television father?
    a. Tom Bosley
    b. Carol O'Connor
    c. Robert Reed
    d. Jamie Fox

16. ★★ Find the beige advertisement with the red writing within this store. What famous item does Minnie sell according to this advertisement?
    a. Brownies
    b. Ice cream
    c. Hamburgers
    d. Pies

17. ★★★ Just above the Minnie's pies advertisement you will find a row of celebrity photos. Which famous actress from the golden age of Hollywood appears in the second photo from the right?
    a. Elizabeth Taylor
    b. Jean Harlow
    c. Marylin Monroe
    d. Jayne Mansfield

The Great Walt Disney World Scavenger Hunt

Adrian and Edith's

18. ★ Enter this shop and take a look at the movie posters above you. What is Pluto's number in the cartoon *Society Dog Show*?
    a. 13
    b. 15
    c. 12
    d. 31

19. ★★ Finish the name of this classic Walt Disney cartoon, "*The Reluctant _____.*"
    a. Bull
    b. Dog
    c. Mouse
    d. Dragon

20. ★ Find the movie poster for the Walt Disney classic *Bambi*. What word means to fall in love?
    a. Head over heels
    b. Twitterpated
    c. Fluttersilly
    d. Twitchy

21. ★ Find the movie poster for *Fantasia*. What animal appears on this poster with Sorcerer Mickey?
    a. Alligator
    b. Hippo
    c. Flamingo
    d. Ostrich

Did you know?

The name of this shop, Adrian and Edith is a nod to two very famous costume designers from Hollywood. Adrian designed costumes for such classic films as *Grand Hotel*, *Ziegfeld Girl* and *The Wizard of Oz*.

Edith Head designed for the films *Barefoot in the Park*, *The Sting*, *Blue Hawaii* and *Funny Face*. She was brought to life in the film *The Incredibles* with the character of Edna Mode who designs the super hero costumes.

The Brown Derby

> **Did you know?**
> The photo's in the gold frames are original from The Brown Derby restaurant in Los Angeles. All others are reproductions of the original works of art.

22. ✯✯✯ As you enter the lobby of The Brown Derby restaurant, stop for a moment to look at the map of Los Angeles on the wall of the waiting area. Which of these is the correct address of the original Brown Derby restaurant?
    a. 12305 Fifth Helena Drive
    b. 8433 Sunset Boulevard
    c. 6667 Hollywood Blvd
    d. 3377 Wilshire Blvd

23. ✯✯✯ As you look at the celebrity caricatures around you, notice the grouping to the left of the doorway. Which famous Broadway and Hollywood actress adorns the frame in the bottom row, fourth from the right?
    a. Julie Andrews
    b. Carol Channing
    c. Barbara Streisand
    d. Chita Rivera

24. ✯✯✯ As you continue to look over these frames, you will notice the star with the Mickey Mouse ears on. Which actor was the leader of the original Mickey Mouse club?
    a. Cubby O'Brien
    b. Bobby Burgess
    c. Roy Williams
    d. Jimmie Dodd

Bonus Question

25. ✯✯✯ If you look directly above the doorway to the restaurant seating area, you will see a frame with Edgar

The Great Walt Disney World Scavenger Hunt

Bergen and two of his famous puppets. One of these puppets is Charlie McCarthy, what is the name of the other shown?

a. Mortimer Snerd
b. Jerry Mahoney
c. Danny O'Day
d. Lester

26. ★★★ As you stand at the corner of Hollywood Blvd and Sunset Blvd, take a moment to look at the map on the corner behind the Disney Vacation Club kiosk. According to the Pacific Electric Railway, how many trains run daily?

a. 5
b. 2700
c. 1000
d. 7200

Sunset Blvd

Join the nightlife of Sunset Blvd as you walk this famous street. Visit the famous Hollywood Tower Hotel and ride into the Twilight Zone™. Get to the concert through Hollywood freeways with Aerosmith or visit with your favorite friends from *Beauty and the Beast* before ending your night with a performance of Fantasmic.

1. ✯✯✯ On the street you will find two sets of luggage waiting for their owners. What is the company that made this luggage?
    a. Samsonite
    b. Traveler's Club
    c. American Tourister
    d. Neiman Marcus

2. ✯✯✯ As you read the luggage tags, you will see this luggage belongs to Gilbert London and Carolyn Crosson. What Disney film are these two names associated with?
    a. The Haunted Mansion
    b. Pirates of the Caribbean
    c. National Treasure
    d. Tower of Terror

Rockin' Roller Coaster Starring Aerosmith

3. ✯✯ As you are standing in the recording studio with Aerosmith, who bursts in to tell them they are late for their show?
    a. Their manager
    b. The studio owner
    c. The club owner
    d. Joe Perry

4. ✯✯✯ What does Joe ask Chris to grab for him over the studio microphone just before the band leaves for the concert?
    a. Blue scarf
    b. Black leather jacket
    c. Red Fender Stratocaster
    d. Black Les Paul

5. ✯✯ As you enter the alley and are waiting for your limo, look at the dumpster across from you. What does the warning label tell you not to do?
    a. Do not ride
    b. Do not climb
    c. Do not play
    d. Do not enter

Did you know?

There are several different Aerosmith songs that play for the different coasters. Ride more than once to experience this attraction with a different soundtrack.

Did you know?

The imagineers left their initials around the queue and load area. Look at some of the electrical boxes to see these memento's.

6. ★★ As you come around the alley in the queue notice the call box next to the cast member. If you dial zero, who will you be calling?
   a. The police
   b. A tow truck
   c. Buses
   d. Parking attendant

7. ★★ Read the menu for the Wash this Way auto detailing. What do you get for $125.00?
   a. Wheel and Deal
   b. Street Emotion detail
   c. Hollywood & Shine
   d. Wash N Roll Wax

8. ★★ What is *not* included along with the tax on the Wash This Way menu?
   a. A big tip
   b. Recycling fees
   c. Soap and water
   d. SUV's

9. ★★ As you enter your limo and are on your way, what Los Angeles exit is on the overpass sign you drive under?
   a. Griffith Park
   b. Hollywood & Highland
   c. Dolby Theater
   d. Civic center

10. ★★ What sort of food does the "All-night" sign offer?
    a. Coffee
    b. Subs
    c. Donuts
    d. Ice cream

Twilight Zone Tower of Terror

11. ★★ As you enter the Hollywood Tower Hotel property, in what year was the Sunset Hills Estates established?
    a. 1928
    b. 1955
    c. 1977
    d. 1921

The Great Walt Disney World Scavenger Hunt

12. ★★ Stop for a moment to look at the Keep Out sign on the front gates. As of what date is this property off limits?
    a. October 31, 1929
    b. October 31, 1939
    c. October 31, 1955
    d. October 31, 1977

13. ★ As you stand in the lobby of the hotel, what floor is the steam baths located on according to the sign?
    a. Penthouse
    b. Mezzanine
    c. Lower level
    d. Top of the tower

Did you know?

Located within the library on one of the top shelves is the fortune telling machine from the *Twilight Zone* episode *Nick of Time* starring William Shatner.

14. ★★★ As you enter the library, find the writing desk with the lamp. What is the hotel room number of the brass key ring sitting atop this desk?
    a. 809
    b. 108
    c. 708
    d. 908

15. ★★★ As you look around the library, find a book with the strange writing on the title. What does the translation read on the book cover?
    a. *It's a Good Life*
    b. *The Monsters are Due on Maple Street*
    c. *To Serve Man*
    d. *Time Enough at Last*

16. ★★ As you exit the library to the boiler room, which of these is not on the sign posted on the wall opposite the doorway?
    a. Pool
    b. Laundry room
    c. Maintenance
    d. Boiler room

> ### Did you know?
> Located within the boiler room, you will find a chalk mark in the shape of a doorway from the Twilight Zone episode *Little Girl Lost*. If you stand here and listen carefully, you can hear Carol Ann call for her mother.

17. ★★★ As you wind your way through the boiler room you will see a workbench with a fan and a pipe resting on it. As you read the card on this table, finish the quote, "It's easy enough to be pleasant, when life hums along like a song. But the man worthwhile is the man who can smile when everything goes _____ wrong."
    a. Totally
    b. Dead
    c. Completely
    d. Plum

18. ★★ As you exit your attraction to go back to the lobby, stop for a moment at a door to the restricted area. What hotel service does extension 8855 ring?
    a. Imagineering
    b. Room service
    c. Engineering
    d. Hotel operator

19. ★★ Stop for a moment at the cage for the maintenance department. On the wall pinned to the cork board you will find a card for Alberton Realty. What is drawn on the front of this card?
    a. A telephone
    b. A wench
    c. A radio
    d. A lightbulb

20. ★★★ Notice the calendar with the boy and his dog on the wall. What company sent this calendar out?
    a. Health insurance
    b. Auto insurance
    c. Main street bank
    d. Auto club

21. ★ As you look at the shelves within the cage, notice the one with several irons. There is a black and yellow box with writing on it. What does this box contain?
    a. Whiskey
    b. Brandy
    c. Stout Ale
    d. Pickled eggs

22. ★ As you look among the jars of cleaners and paint, there is an unusual wooden box. What does this box contain according to the label?
    a. Apples
    b. Bananas
    c. Cherries
    d. Dates

23. ★★ Stop for a moment to read the menu for the Halloween dinner in the Sunset Room. Which of these is *not* one of the items listed under Hors D 'oeuvres?
    a. Bismark Herrings
    b. Sweet Gherkins a la Moutarde
    c. Quail eggs on Toast Points
    d. Grape Fruit Maraschino

Did you know?

Spend some time looking in the case at the artifacts beneath the Tower of Terror pictures. Notice the gold thimble from the Twilight Zone episode *The After Hours*. Search the top shelves of the gift shop and you will find the doll Talky Tina from the *Living Doll* episode.

Carthay Circle

24. ★★★ As you enter the store for Carthay Circle, notice the photographs around the room. Find the picture of Walt Disney, who is the woman in the picture with him?
    a. Sharon Disney
    b. Julie Andrews
    c. Lillian Disney
    d. Marilyn Monroe

> ### Did you know?
> This shop is named for the Carthay Circle theater in Los Angeles where the first full length Walt Disney animated film *Snow White and the Seven Dwarves* premiered.

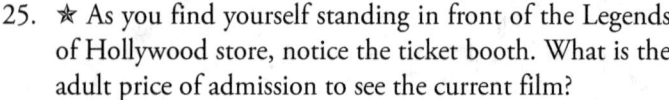

25. ★ As you find yourself standing in front of the Legends of Hollywood store, notice the ticket booth. What is the adult price of admission to see the current film?
    a. 35 cents
    b. 25 cents
    c. 50 cents
    d. 95 cents

Echo Lake

Join old Hollywood around Echo Lake as you are in front of the action with Indiana Jones in the exciting stunt spectacular. Have lunch at the 50's Prime Time Café or get something cool with Gertie the Dinosaur.

> ### Did you know?
> Find the umbrellas next to the green building. Above these you will find the advertisement for Eddie Valiant, Private Investigator. This is a reference to the film *Who Framed Roger Rabbit* including the broken window in the shape of Roger where he left the office after finding out his wife, Jessica, played patty cake with another man.

50's Prime Time Cafe

1. ★ As you enter the 50's Prime Time Café, take a look around the living room, what statue set rests on top of the radio?
    a. Matador and Bull
    b. Tango dancers
    c. King and Queen
    d. Boy And his dog

2. ★★ Take a look at the book shelves in the living room area and find the Childcraft books, what subject does volume 10 teach?
   a. Science
   b. Art
   c. Music
   d. Nature

3. ★★★ As you look at the book bindings, find the red book for *Oliver Twist*. Who is the author of this classic novel?
   a. Mark Twain
   b. Lewis Carroll
   c. Charles Dickens
   d. Kenneth Grahame

4. ★★ Stop in the kitchen and look at the cake pans hanging above. What decoration adorns the cake pan on the far left?
   a. Fish
   b. Flowers
   c. A Turkey
   d. Grapes

5. ★ What brand name is shown on the front of the refrigerator in the kitchen?
   a. Frigidaire
   b. WED
   c. General Electric
   d. Amana

6. ★ As you walk down the hallway to the restrooms, you will find several framed pictures. What famous classic television show is shown with a group on the golf course?
   a. *I Love Lucy*
   b. *The Honeymooners*
   c. *Father Knows Best*
   d. *Leave it to Beaver*

7. ★ As you wander through the 50's Prime Time Café, you will find a set of white containers, which of these is *not* one of the labels on these canisters?
   a. Coffee
   b. Tea
   c. Rice
   d. Flour

The Great Walt Disney World Scavenger Hunt

8. ★★ Now find the calendar on the wall with the picture of the baseball game. What month and year is this calendar showing?
   a. April, 1977
   b. April, 1952
   c. April, 1955
   d. April, 1925

9. ★★ Now find the ceramic trolley on the shelf within the restaurant. What is this trolley used for?
   a. Cookies
   b. Chips
   c. Crackers
   d. Crumbs

10. ★ As you exit the restaurant and look across at the giant dinosaur on the lake, what is the name of this dinosaur?
    a. Dink
    b. Dino
    c. Gertie
    d. Rex

11. ★★ Find the plaque commemorating the original films about this dinosaur. What style of architecture is this structure called?
    a. Early American
    b. California Crazy
    c. Chinese Modern
    d. Neoclassic Baroque

Did you know?

The original cartoon for Gertie the Dinosaur was created in 1914. In 1991, the Library of Congress selected this animated film for the national film registry.

12. ★★ Find the gates for the Echo Lake Apartments. As you read the mailboxes, what name is on the box in the upper right corner?

a.	Mr. & Mrs. D. Yancer	c.	T. Kirk
b.	Beyer/Quinn	d.	Polk/Olsen

> ### Did you know?
> The names on the mailboxes in front of Echo Lake Apartments are the names of Imagineers with the Walt Disney Company.

13. ★★ Just above the Hollywood and Vine buffet you will find a for rent poster in the window. What sort of people will they *not* rent to?
    - a. Actors
    - b. Animators
    - c. Cartoons
    - d. Californians

14. ★★★ Look for the billboard for Maroon Cartoons. Who is featured on this billboard along with Roger and Jessica Rabbit?
    - a. Eddie Valiant
    - b. Dr. Doom
    - c. Mickey Mouse
    - d. Baby Herman

Indiana Jones Epic Stunt Spectacular!

> ### Did you know?
> Arrive early for this show and you could be chosen as one of the extras for this show. Keep in mind, the casting director is looking for high energy people who want to have fun.

> ### Did you know?
>
> As you walk through the queue before entering the amphitheater you will find a well with a sign "Do not pull rope". Feel free to indulge yourself and pull the rope. You will hear the archeologists below calling to you.

> ### Did you know?
>
> George Lucas attended the first performance of the Indiana Jones Epic Stunt Spectacular and gave his approval to the show as a great representation of the film.

Star Tours – The Adventure Continues

15. ★★ As you enter the queue for Star Tours, note the large figure above you. What is the name of this machine from the *Star Wars* films?
    a. Vulture Droid
    b. V19 Torrent
    c. At At
    d. Hornet Interceptor

16. ★★★ As you enter the building, look at the window above you. Which Star Wars character is sitting at the control panel?
    a. Admiral Ackbar
    b. General Grievous
    c. Chewbacca
    d. Obi Wan Kenobi

17. ★★ As you read the display for the flights, what is the status of flight 810 from Naboo?
    a. Landed
    b. Gate change
    c. Gate closed
    d. On time

18. ★★ Flight 1009 is arriving from Storinal, what is the status of this flight?

a. Delayed
b. Cancelled
c. On approach
d. Boarding

19. ★★ If you listen to the announcements throughout the terminal, what is required of all droids leaving the system?
    a. Checked for bugs
    b. Cleared by customs
    c. Memory wiped
    d. New control chips be installed

20. ★★★ Work your way around to the luggage droid who is scanning your suitcases. What obscure musical instrument is found in one of the bags?
    a. Ukulele
    b. A Theremin
    c. Harpsicord
    d. Bag pipes

21. ★★★ As the scanner droid continues his work, you will see a costume from which Pixar film?
    a. *The Incredibles*
    b. *Monster's University*
    c. *Toy Story*
    d. *Cars*

22. ★★ What is GQ9B's response to the alarm going off?
    a. "Intruder Alert"
    b. "What do I do?"
    c. "How do I get out of here?"
    d. "Where's the snooze bar?"

23. ★★ Why would people try to smuggle droids according to GQ9B?
    a. One less carry on item
    b. To avoid paying duty fees
    c. So they don't get taken
    d. No reason

24. ★★★ What toy from the Pixar film *Toy Story* is seen by the scanner?
    a. Sherriff Woody
    b. Rex
    c. Buzz Lightyear
    d. Slinky Dog

25. ★★ As you continue in the queue, stop for a moment at the droid just before boarding. What is it that Mike has done to cause an alert?
    a. Sold secrets to the empire
    b. Selling defective lightsabers
    c. Stole an X-wing fighter
    d. Driving a star speeder without a license

Did you know?

Don't miss Jedi Training: Trials of the Temple. This attraction is available for the little guests only. Be sure to schedule this into your day and sign up first thing in the morning as this show fills up quickly each day.

Did you know?

In another part of the park is the Star Wars Launch Bay, an interactive experience where you can meet Chewbacca, Kylo Ren and other characters from your favorite *Star Wars* films.

Grand Avenue

Play along with Kermit the Frog, Miss Piggy and Fozzie Bear as you join the cast of The Muppets for some fun and frolic. Get a bite at Mama Melrose Restaurant Italiano or with Rizzo at his pizza place. Before you go, don't miss a change to get an authentic souvenir from the set of *The Great Muppet Caper* or *The Muppet Movie*.

1. ★★ In the center of the courtyard you will find a large fountain, which Muppet character is the camera man?
    a. Kermit the Frog
    b. Miss Piggy
    c. Fozzie Bear
    d. Sam the Eagle

2. ★ If you look closely at the rats in the fountain, what are they fishing for?
    a. Fish
    b. Cheese
    c. Spare change
    d. Their rat friends

Muppet Vision 3D

3. ★★★ Which Muppet character can be seen to the left of the entrance with the Muppet Vision sign?
    a. Big Bird
    b. Sweetums
    c. Dr. Teeth
    d. Animal

The Great Walt Disney World Scavenger Hunt

4. ★★★ As you enter Muppetvision 3-D stop at the security area for a moment. Look for the picture of the officer on duty, which Muppet character do you see?
   a. Link Hogthrob
   b. Dr. Strangepork
   c. Captain Blueboar
   d. Warthog

> ### Did you know?
> At security, find the sign that reads, "Back in 5 Minutes, the key is under the mat." Look under the mat and you will find a key.

> ### Did you know?
> Look up at the arch you walk under as you leave security. Someone has written "You must be shorter than this to enter." Notice the large chunk taken out of the wall just below this writing.

5. ★ As you read the directory for Muppet Vision 3-D World Headquarters, read the Kitchen & Pyrotechnics research departments. What official title does the Swedish Chef have?
   a. Chef at large
   b. Yummy yummy tummy cook
   c. Tippy top cookie guy
   d. No one else wanted it

6. ★ What department is Miss Piggy head of according to the directory?
   a. Academy of amphibian science
   b. Attitudinal adjustment
   c. Department of diva screams
   d. Sartorial accumulation division

> **Did you know?**
> Read the doors as you work your way down the corridor. The Muppet labs has some very interesting departments.

7. ★★ As you look around the large wooden boxes in the back-stage area, stop for a moment to read the container with the portrait of Rowlf the dog. What is the portrait called that is in this container?
   a. A dog's life
   b. Escape from the pound
   c. My life as a mutt
   d. Furry furry little pup

8. ★★ Find the large crate addressed to Mr. Fozzie Bear from Mr. Bellylaff's of Encino. Which of these items is *not* included in this box?
   a. Rubber toast
   b. Ten tiny tin toy boats
   c. Non-dairy cream pies
   d. Barnyard noisemakers

9. ★★ Find the crate with the descending stair case addressed to the Great Gonzo. What is the name of the production using Gonzo's descending stair case?
   a. Stair Trek
   b. Stair Wars
   c. A Stair is Born
   d. Down the up staircase

10. ★★ Which store has sent Scooter a large wooden crate of glasses?
    a. The glasses store (Not to be confused with the other glasses store)
    b. The Glassed and the Furious
    c. Spanky's Spectacular Spectacles
    d. Lady Ga-goggles

11. ★★ Beneath the large red box of the Great Gonzo's stunt props is a small box addressed to Kermit the Frog. What is contained in this box?
    a. Mickey Mouse watch
    b. Formal wedding tuxedo from Miss Piggy
    c. Banjo's
    d. Neck Ruffs

Bonus Question

12. ★★★ As you look at the rafters above your head you will see a silver space ship. What was the name of the sketch on *The Muppet Show* this prop was used in?
    a. The three little pigs in space
    b. Pig's in Space
    c. Swine Trek
    d. Pig's on the Moon

> **Did you know?**
>
> As you look around the props you will see a large net above your head with what appear to be cubes in it. This is a nod to Mouseketeer Annette Funicello, A net full of Jell-O.

13. ★ As the pre-show video begins, you see a group of construction workers walk into the screen. What sort of animal is Chuck?
    a. Dog
    b. Cat
    c. Penguin
    d. Human

14. ★ As you see the worker painting the Background on the television screen, what appears as he is painting?
    a. An aquarium
    b. A mountain range
    c. A studio backlot
    d. A stage and scenery

> ### Did you know?
> Notice the large musical instrument the penguin is holding on the right side of the screen. This instrument is commonly called a tuba. This is in fact called a Sousaphone, named after the great composer John Philip Sousa.

15. ★★★ Which Muppet performer helps Scooter get the people quiet to hear his announcement?
    a. Gonzo
    b. Sweetums
    c. Floyd
    d. Rizzo

16. ★★ What is the name of the third girl introduced in the Three Dee's?
    a. Delores
    b. Destiny
    c. Max
    d. Daphne

Bonus Question

17. ★★★ As the video feed is interrupted we see Constantine, the bad guy. Which Muppet film was this character introduced to audiences?
    a. *Muppets Take Manhattan*
    b. *The Great Muppet Caper*
    c. *The Muppet Movie*
    d. *Muppets Most Wanted*

18. ★ Which famous Disney character does Rizzo the rat try to pretend to be?
    a. Cruella De Vil
    b. Mickey Mouse
    c. Donald Duck
    d. Snow White

The Great Walt Disney World Scavenger Hunt

> **Did you know?**
>
> As you enter the theater for the main show, stop for a moment to look around you. Notice the statuary throughout the theater are your favorite Muppet characters

19. ✯✯ As you hear Statler and Waldorf chatting, why do they say the penguins took this job?
    a. No work in the arctic
    b. For the halibut
    c. No one else would take the job
    d. They already owned tuxedos

20. ✯✯ As Kermit the Frog takes you on a tour of Muppet Labs, what sort of live animal do you see wandering in the background?
    a. Chickens
    b. Cats
    c. Bunnies
    d. Frogs

21. ✯✯ As we enter the secret lab of Dr. Bunsen Honeydew, what do you see Beaker doing?
    a. Mixing potions
    b. Fixing the equipment
    c. Dusting
    d. Eating lunch

22. ✯ What sort of remote-controlled item does Fozzie Bear invent?
    a. Squirting flower
    b. Whoopee cushion
    c. Coconut cream pie
    d. Banana cream pie

23. ✯✯✯ As bean bunny runs away from Muppet Labs and the crew start to look for him, which character do you see coming out into the theater in front of you?
    a. Fozzie Bear
    b. Sam Eagle
    c. Sweetums
    d. The Swedish Chef

> ### Did you know?
> As the finale begins and the Sousaphone gets stuck on the performers head, listen very carefully. You will hear *It's a Small World* being sung for only a few seconds.

24. ★★★ Which Muppet character fires the cannon that blows up the theater you are sitting in?
    a. Swedish Chef
    b. Crazy Harry
    c. Uncle Deadly
    d. Count von Count

> ### Did you know?
> As you watch the fire truck enter the brick wall, notice the license plate. It is the castle logo for the Walt Disney company. Also, note the tourists with the Mickey balloons looking into the wreckage.

Stage 1 Company Store

> ### Did you know?
> Look above your head and you will find a camera with a director's chair beside it. Mr. The Frog adorns the back of this chair as a nod to director Kermit the Frog.

25. ★ Find the Safety-First sign within Stage 1 Company Store. How many days have they gone without an accident?
    a. 999
    b. 10
    c. 2
    d. Zero

The Great Walt Disney World Scavenger Hunt

26. ★★ Find the sign that reads "Through these halls pass the most talented performers in the business." Who wrote these words?
    a. Manager
    b. Agent
    c. Accountant
    d. Director

27. ★★★ Find the sign for the five laws of show business. Which of these is number five?
    a. The star is always right
    b. There's no such thing as net profits
    c. The writer is always wrong
    d. The audience is always right

Bonus question:

28. ★★★ As you approach the set for the Happiness Hotel, what is the name of the flag you see hanging from the second floor?
    a. Grand 'Ol Flag
    b. Star Spangled Banner
    c. Union Jack
    d. Southern Cross Flag

29. ★★ As you read the signs around the check in desk, what do the management encourage you to steal?
    a. Food
    b. Everything
    c. Rats
    d. Linen

30. ★★ As you continue exploring the set from the happiness hotel, what sort of beds do they feature?
    a. Water bed
    b. Hammocks
    c. Flower bed
    d. Murphy bed

31. ★★ As you continue your exploration of Stage 1, you will find a sign posted on the wall, "Absolutely no _____, this mean you!" What is the missing word?

a.	Solicitors	c.	Visitors
b.	Luggage	d.	Food or drink

32. ★★ Before you exit this store, stop at the bus station set. Find the green jar on the shelf, what does the label on this jar read?
    - a. Jam
    - b. Hunny
    - c. Doc Hopper's deep-fried frog legs
    - d. Flies

33. ★★★ Find the sticker on the round red suitcase in the bus station set. What hotel is this sticker from?
    - a. Cactus motel
    - b. Happiness hotel
    - c. Grand Floridian hotel
    - d. M. Mouse hotel

34. ★★ Who is the manufacturer of the green suitcase sitting on top of the round red suitcase on the shelf?
    - a. American Tourister
    - b. Caperlite
    - c. Samsonite
    - d. Tough flight

Bonus question:

35. ★★★ What famous magician's picture is pasted to one of the openings you see in the lockers?
    - a. Copperfield
    - b. Henning
    - c. Houdini
    - d. The great Rizzo

36. ★ Read the warning sign and finish this sentence, "Trespassers will be _____."
    - a. Arrested
    - b. Used as extras
    - c. Turned over to Animal
    - d. Ventilated

> **Did you know?**
>
> Outside Stage 1 Company Store you will find a series of pipes painted a variety of bright colors. These pipes are a nod to the Muppet artists. In 1964, Jim Henson, Frank Oz and several other Muppet artists were scheduled to appear on the Jack Paar show in New York's NBC studios.
>
> Not only did NBC save the pipes from being painted over or removed during renovations, the pipes are now part of the NBC tour and have been preserved behind glass to remain forever as a memorial to this famous story.

Mama Melrose Ristorante Italiano

37. ★ As you approach Mama Melrose Ristorante Italiano, take a look at the window above. What is the name of the magic shop?
    a. Abracadabra
    b. Hocus Pocus
    c. Now you see it, now you don't
    d. The Amazing Mumford

38. ★★★ Find the large mural for Mama Melrose outside the restaurant. What famous painting is parodied on this mural?
    a. Madonna on the Rocks
    b. The Mona Lisa
    c. Birth of Venus
    d. The Last Supper

39. ★ As you take a tour of the restaurant, find the wall with the mounted fish with yellow sunglasses. On this wall you will find a bumper sticker. According to this sticker, what is a fine Italian name?
    a. America
    b. Italy
    c. Giuseppe
    d. Mama

40. ★★ Find the wall with the I love L.A. license plate. Below you will find a record album cover. What is the name of the artist featured on this cover?
    a. Frank Sinatra
    b. Julius LaRosa
    c. Guy Lombardo
    d. Mel Torme

Did you know?

As you continue your tour of Mama Melrose, you will find a pizza on the wall with eight pizza slices around it. The decorators have created a sun shape out of the pizza slices.

---

41. ★★★ Find the Spaghetti & Co. poster. How many different types of pasta do you see on this poster?
    a. 41
    b. 55
    c. 61
    d. 51

42. ★★ Find the map of Italy with the name Vini Ditalia. What does the mermaid hold in her hand at the bottom of this poster?
    a. A trident
    b. A glass of wine
    c. A plate of spaghetti
    d. A fish

43. ★ Outside Mama Melrose Ristorante Italiano, you will find a tomato loading zone. Finish the small sign to the left of this doorway, "No parking, no standing, no stopping _____."
    a. No kidding
    b. No sitting
    c. No eating
    d. No joking

> **Did you know?**
> Look closely at the Tomato Loading Zone sign, you will notice tomatoes have been thrown at the door and sign.

> **Did you know?**
> Next door to Mama Melrose is the Engine Company No. 1, the fire department for Muppet Courtyard. Look at the fire escape above to see the fire hose draped over the rails.

PizzeRizzo

44. ★★ Find the plaque for the PizzeRizzo Pizza Eating Contest Hall of Fame. How many times did Big Mean Carl win?
    a. 1   c. 9
    b. 6   d. 8

45. ★★ Which Muppet won the 6th annual pizza eating contest?
    a. Sweetums   c. Animal
    b. Big Mean Carl   d. Fozzie bear

> **Did you know?**
> Read the side of the trash cans, Rizzo left a message telling patrons to clean up after themselves, your mama don't work here.

46. ★ Find the subway sign for the 18th Street station within PizzeRizzo. This link goes to uptown and what New York borough?

a. Bronx   c. Manhattan
b. Brooklyn   d. Staten Island

47. ★★★ Head upstairs to the second floor. Among the framed record albums, you will find one entitled The Longhorn Cheddar Cheese's. What is the fourth song on this album?
    a. Bleu Moon
    b. Fromage in Low Places
    c. I'll Treat you Cheddar
    d. What Cheese Doing Now

48. ★★★ In a quiet corner of the restaurant, you will find a cork board with several notices. What sort of juggler is for hire?
    a. Fish
    b. Fire
    c. Bowling ball
    d. Muppet

49. ★★★ Find the advertisement for the banquet hall. According to the notice, the hall holds 150 guests or how many rats?
    a. 758
    b. 785
    c. 578
    d. 875

> ### Did you know?
> On the second floor of PizzeRizzo's, you can eat in the ballroom complete with mirror ball and fabric bunting decorated for your next event.

50. ★★ As you walk through Muppet courtyard, find a set of double doors painted blue. Above these doors, which Muppets character has written the Props Department on the wall?
    a. Rizzo
    b. Fozzie
    c. Kermit
    d. Animal

Star Wars: Galaxy's Edge

Arrive on an outpost on the edge of the universe to have your own Star Wars adventure when you explore Star Wars: Galaxy's Edge at Disney Hollywood Studios.

Ride the biggest hunk of junk in the galaxy or escape from the First Order. Come face to face with your favorite Star Wars characters and villains as they walk among the guests at Black Spire Outpost.

1. ★★ When you enter Star Wars: Galaxy's Edge from Toy Story Land, you will see several vehicles within a cover area to the left edge. What is the name of the brown speeder with the blue accents?
   a. Starspeeder
   b. Lightspeeder
   c. Landspeeder
   d. Rebel Speeder

Did you know?

Look at the ground as you work your way through the Black Spire Outpost. You will see droid tracks as well as creature footprints as you go along.

> ### Did you know?
> Listen carefully as you spend time within Star Wars: Galaxy's Edge. You will hear creatures in the shrubs and space crafts flying and landing high above your head.

> ### Did you know?
> Watch out for Kylo Ren or the Stormtroopers wandering through the crowd looking for a rebel spy. If they stop you, be prepared to answer questions about your activities in the outpost.

> ### Did you know?
> Guests can build their own R or BB unit here at the Droid Depot for only $99 credits. For those with a bigger budget, you can even purchase a full size fully operational R2D2 unit.

2. ★★ Find the Milk Stand and purchase either the blue or green milk. What creature from the Star Wars universe does the green milk come from?
   a. Wampa
   b. Thala-siren
   c. Bergruutfa
   d. Porg

> ### Did you know?
> Download the Play Disney app and scan the crates around Black Spire Outpost. Your app will disclose the contents of the crates. You may find some very familiar items within from the Star Wars universe.

The Great Walt Disney World Scavenger Hunt

Oga's Cantina

3. ★★★ Before you enter Oga's Cantina, you will need to translate the code of conduct. Finish this sentence, "No fighting, biting or _____."
   a. Tearing off of limbs
   b. Shooting
   c. Light Sabers
   d. Smuggling

4. ★★★ According to the code of conduct, how many drinks are Wookiees limited to?
   a. 5
   b. 10
   c. 1
   d. 2

5. ★★★ What is the name of the D.J. droid you find spinning tunes for the guests?
   a. C3PO
   b. R2D2
   c. AZI-3
   d. R3X

Did you know?

The D.J. at Oga's Cantina may look familiar to guests who have rode Star Tours. This little droid was the pilot of the Starspeeder 3000.

Millennium Falcon: Smugglers Run

Did you know?

Stand in front of the Millennium Falcon and get your picture taken. From time to time, the falcon will light up and steam will escape from the hull showing the wear and tear on this hardworking craft.

6. ★★ As you work your way through the queue for the Millennium Falcon, look to your left and find a storage

area. There is a card game sitting atop a makeshift table, what is the name of this game?

a. Battlefront
b. Cabbal
c. Sabacc
d. Smugglers poker

Did you know?

As you look around the storage area, you may recognize weapons, helmets, flight suits and even a bomb from the Star Wars universe.

---

7. ★ As you enter the Falcon and wait for your time in the cockpit, sit at the Dejarik table. What is this game more commonly known as?

a. Holocheckers
b. Holochess
c. Wookiee Chess
d. Jedi Checkers

Did you know?

Sitting on a shelf behind the Dejarik seating area is a small box with an orb inside. Guests may recognize this as the orb used to train Luke Skywalker on the Millennium Falcon.

---

8. ★ As you enter the load area for your ride, listen to Ohnaka tell you about your mission. What items will you be stealing from the transport?

a. Gold
b. Princess Leia
c. Kyber crystals
d. Coaxium

Did you know?

Millennium Falcon Smugglers Run is a fully interactive experience. Pilots will move the Falcon through space while the gunners shoot and the engineers capture the cargo.

The Great Walt Disney World Scavenger Hunt

> **Did you know?**
>
> As you exit the Millennium Falcon through the tunnels, look around. You may recognize the red doors on either side of the passage as storage areas for Rathtar cargo as seen in Star Wars Episode VII - The Force Awakens.

Dok-Ondar's Den of Antiquities

9. ★★ As you enter Dok-Ondar's Den of Antiquities, look up to the second level and you will find a large full-size white creature. What is the name of this creature?
    a. Wampa
    b. Tauntaun
    c. Wookiee
    d. Polar Skew

10. ★★★ Look very carefully at the second level and you will find a gold mask lying atop a chest. Which Star Wars characters face does this mask depict?
    a. Chewbacca
    b. Han Solo
    c. Jar Jar Binx
    d. Darth Vader

> **Did you know?**
>
> Hidden on the second level of Dok-Ondar's you will find a golden chest hidden behind several other items. This chest is the Ark of the Covenant from *Raiders of the Lost Ark* starring Han Solo actor Harrison Ford.

> **Did you know?**
>
> If you look up at the medal hanging high up behind the sales counter, you may recognize this item as the medal Princess Leia presents to Han Solo, Luke Skywalker and Chewbacca in *Star Wars – A New Hope*.

> ### Did you know?
> Near the entrance to Dok-Ondar's Den of Antiquities, guests will find a very quiet area at the bottom of a set of stairs. Could this be where Jedi's create their own light sabers to join the force as the next generation of Jedi warriors?

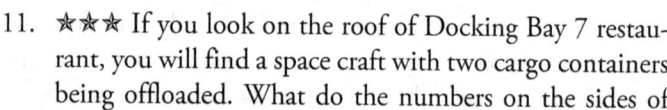

11. ★★★ If you look on the roof of Docking Bay 7 restaurant, you will find a space craft with two cargo containers being offloaded. What do the numbers on the sides of these containers reference in the Star Wars universe?
    a. The ages of Luke Skywalker and Han Solo
    b. Reference to the cargo inside
    c. The number of Star Wars films to date
    d. The years the first three Star Wars films were released

12. ★★ Find Ronto Roasters and notice the way the food is being cooked. What is the large blue heating device being used?
    a. Star Destroyer engine
    b. Millennium Falcon engine
    c. Podracer engine
    d. Landspeeder engine

13. ★★★ Find the toy shop in the market place. What is the name of the Star Wars characters shown on the sign outside this stall?
    a. Kylo
    b. Watto
    c. Jabba
    d. Anakin

> ### Did you know?
> Look around the Toydarian Toy stall and you will see Obi Wan Kenobi fighting Darth Vader and a Star Destroyer battle hanging from the ceiling.
>   Also, guests will see the Toydarian hard at work behind frosted glass.

14. ★★★ Across from the Toydarian stall, guests will find the creature stall. What is the name of the creature in the cage in the center of the stall?
    a. Loth-cat
    b. Kowakian monkey lizard
    c. Wampa
    d. Mynock

> ### Did you know?
> As you look around the creature stall, you may notice glowing eyes staring back at you from the cages with tags hanging from them. Some are hanging from above while there is at least one at eye level.

15. ★★★ At the end of the market stalls, guests will find a drinking fountain. What is the name of the creature you see looking at you from the tank above the fountain?
    a. Mynock
    b. Rathtar
    c. Krykna Spider
    d. Dianoga

Star Wars: Rise of the Resistance

16. ★ When you enter the first room in the resistance bunker, which droid greets you?
    a. R2D2
    b. C3PO
    c. BB8
    d. K-2SO

17. ★★ Which Star Wars character leads you to the secret base?
    a. Finn
    b. Lt. Beck
    c. Poe
    d. Rey

18. ★★ As you are loading your transport, listen to the overhead announcement. What item is there no need for?
    a. Safety gear
    b. Training
    c. Blasters
    d. Flight plan

19. ★★ As the Lieutenant is confirming that everyone is ready to go, finish this line, "Red 2, blue _____ report."
    a. Six
    b. Five
    c. Seven
    d. Nine

20. ★ When Lieutenant Beck tells them to raise the shields, what sort of craft is approaching your transport?
    a. X wing fighters
    b. Star destroyers
    c. Land speeders
    d. Tie fighters

21. ★★ When Lieutenant Beck asks by what authority we are being boarded, what name does the first order commander call him?
    a. Rebel filth
    b. Rebel disease
    c. Rebel Scum
    d. Rebel junk

Did you know?

When Lieutenant Beck says, "I have a bad feeling about this." This line is well known in the Star Wars universe said by different Star Wars characters throughout the film franchise.

22. ★★ As you are loaded into the ride vehicle, what sort of droid almost spots you as you move through the Star Destroyer?

a.	Clone trooper	c.	At
b.	Battle droid	d.	Probe droid

23. ☆ When Kylo Ren is informed the prisoners have escaped, what is his reaction?
    a. How brave
    b. How stupid
    c. How could you be so stupid?
    d. How dare they

Did you know?

You can meet Chewbacca and Rey along the path near Star Wars: Rise of the Resistance.

Toy Story Land

Explore Andy's back yard as you visit with your favorite toys from *Toy Story*. Ride along with Slinky Dog or travel into space with the Buzz Lightyear before stopping for a bite to eat from Woody's Lunch Box. Finish up your time with a thrilling ride on Toy Story Mania before it's back to the toy box for the night.

1. ★ As you find the entrance to Toy Story Land, which of your favorite toys from this iconic movie do you see greeting you?
    a. Buzz Lightyear
    b. Jessie
    c. Bullseye
    d. Woody

2. ★ Find the Toy Story logo on the entrance. What child's toy is this logo printed on?
    a. Rubber ball
    b. Yo yo
    c. Record
    d. Ping pong paddle

3. ★ Woody's arm rest on the word Land spelled out with colored blocks. What color is the letter A?
    a. Blue
    b. Red
    c. Yellow
    d. Green

4. ★★ As you turn into Andy's backyard, you will find a roller coaster towering above. Centered within the coaster you will find Rex the dinosaur standing on what child's toy?
   a. Domino's
   b. Scrabble tiles
   c. Jenga
   d. Dice

Toy Story Mania!

5. ★★ As you stand in front of the Toy Story Midway Mania attraction, look up at the sign. Which Toy Story character is standing in the ticket booth on the right side of the entrance?
   a. Stinky Pete
   b. Wheezy
   c. Jessie
   d. Rex

6. ★★★ As you continue down the path through the queue, you will come to the side of the Toy Story box. Which of these is the correct UPS proof of purchase code?
   a. 789122 610221
   b. 1226102 1220216
   c. 0216102 122789
   d. 122789 0216102

7. ★ To the left of the path you will find two game booths. Which of these prizes does Woody hold in his hands?
   a. Bear
   b. Bunny
   c. Buzz Lightyear
   d. Mr. Potato head

8. ★ As you walk through the box for the Toy Story Play set, which of these items does the box advise you to use to permanently bond the pieces together?
   a. Super glue
   b. Rubber cement
   c. Tape
   d. Paste

9. ★★ As you wind your way through the outdoor queue, you will find several game pieces. Which character do you see on the pink game piece?

    a. Little Miss Muffet   c. Bo Peep
    b. Barbie   d. Buttercup

10. ★★ Before you enter the building, look at the doorway from the FastPass queue. What card game frames the doorway?
    a. Old Maid
    b. Go Fish
    c. Uno
    d. Concentration

11. ★ As you enter the Toy Story Mania building, you will see your favorite characters lining the walls. Which character is playing fortune teller?
    a. Mrs. Potato Head
    b. Bo Peep
    c. Barbie
    d. Mr. Potato Head

12. ★★ Find the View-Master slide sitting between two orange blocks. Which land within the Magic Kingdom is the subject of this disc?
    a. Fantasyland
    b. Tomorrowland
    c. Adventureland
    d. Frontierland

13. ★★ Within the queue, you will find a second View-Master slide for the Disney classic, *Peter Pan*. Read this disc carefully, what period of time was Tinkerbell banished?
    a. 10 days
    b. 3 days
    c. One-month
    d. One week

14. ★★ Find the Rocky Gibraltar toy lifting a dumbbell. What is the weight of the dumbbell he holds?
    a. 1000 lbs.
    b. 500 lbs.
    c. 2000 lbs.
    d. 5000 lbs.

15. ★★ Above your head, find the Candyland board. Near the mountain pass you will find a sign post. How many miles is written on this signpost?
    a. 29
    b. 192
    c. 92
    d. 292

The Great Walt Disney World Scavenger Hunt

16. ★★ Near the Toy Story cutouts on the wall, you will find a game card with the words Lose a Turn printed on it. What fairy tale character adorns this card?
    a. Simple Simon
    b. Little Jack Horner
    c. Jack Sprat
    d. Little Miss Muffet

17. ★★ Near the emergency exit door, you will find a property card from which railroad in the Monopoly game?
    a. Reading Railroad
    b. B & O Railroad
    c. Short Line
    d. Pennsylvania Railroad

18. ★ Taped to the wall, find the Buzz Lightyear maze. What location are you helping Buzz find his way towards?
    a. Interplanetary Diner
    b. Space Carnival
    c. Spaceport
    d. Pizza Planet

19. ★★★ Next to Mr. Potato Head you will find a box of Crayola markers. According to the box, how many crayons does Crayola produce each day?
    a. 3 million
    b. 3 billion
    c. 12 billion
    d. 12 million

20. ★ As you walk around the Lincoln Log building, you will find a pink crayon standing on end. What is the name of this color according to the wrapper?
    a. Bubblegum pink
    b. Baby pink
    c. Bashful pink
    d. Carnation pink

21. ★★ Find the Pumpin' Heart game box. What is the name of the Dr. on the game box?
    a. Dr. Heart attack
    b. Dr. Pumps a lot
    c. Dr. Malpractice
    d. Dr. Beats

22. ★★ Find the hand drawn wanted poster for Mr. Potato Head. What amount is the reward to catch this desperate criminal?
    a. 50 Billion
    b. 50 Bzillion
    c. 5 Billion
    d. 5 Bzillion

23. ★★ As you enter the loading area, look around at the toys. Find the storybook with the boy and his dog, what is the dog's name?
    a. Fido
    b. Spot
    c. Barney
    d. Sydney

24. ★ Find the stack of books on their side in Andy's room, what title does the green book have?
    a. *The Boy Scout Handbook*
    b. *Treasure Island*
    c. *Babes in Toyland*
    d. *Wind in the Willows*

25. ★ As you enter your ride vehicle and see the little golden book, what Pixar short is on the title of this book?
    a. Knick Knack
    b. One Man Band
    c. Presto
    d. Tin Toy

26. ★ What sort of objects are you throwing during your practice game on Toy Story Mania?
    a. Balloons
    b. Darts
    c. Pies
    d. Plates

Did you know?

If you hit the mouse crawling up the side of the barn, you will trigger the barn to rotate 180 degrees. Hit the three mice within the barn and you will open several targets worth more points.

The Great Walt Disney World Scavenger Hunt

Did you know?

As you come to the Dino Darts game, aim for the long balloons at the top of the volcano. After you hit the three long balloons, you will trigger the volcano to erupt balloons.

Did you know?

As you arrive at the army men plate break, hit the two plates that jump up with the 2000-point values. This will open the mountain and a tank will shoot plates at you worth 5000 points each.

Did you know?

At the alien ring toss, hit all of the aliens in the center of the rocket ship. If you make them all disappear at one time, you will trigger a robot to open his mouth for you to shoot rings into for extra points.

Did you know?

When you arrive at Woody's Rootin' Tootin' Shootin' Gallery, hit each target to open them all up. Clear the board and targets worth 1000 and 2000 points will fill the board for you to hit.

Once you finish this part of the board, you will travel along. Hit the targets worth 1000 and 2000 points close to the bottom of the screen.

As the mine cars appear, hit the bat hanging above two times to make the mine cars worth 5000 points each. When the target appears in the finale, hit it as fast as you can to make the target worth more points.

27. ★★ As you exit Toy Story Mania, find a large stack of checkers holding up the checker board to your right. How many checkers are stacked up?
    a. 12
    b. 16
    c. 24
    d. 18

28. ★★ Find the package for Buzz Lightyear Attack on Zurg. The price in the U.S. is $4.95. Which of these choices is the correct price in Canada?
    a. $2.95
    b. $50.00
    c. $14.95
    d. $150.00

29. ★★ According to the box for the Woody's Roundup Western Town Playset, what item will you receive as a bonus with the mail in voucher?
    a. Bullseye's stable
    b. Buzz Lightyear
    c. Stinky Pete's Place
    d. Woody's Sheriff's Station

30. ★★★ As you exit Toy Story Mania, stop to look at the Carnival Cannon. Which of these characters are *not* on a blue target card according to the package?
    a. Wheezy
    b. Slinky Dog
    c. Bullseye
    d. Mrs. Potato Head

31. ★★ As you walk by the Kinex Helicopter building set, how many pieces are contained in this set?
    a. 62 pieces
    b. 52 pieces
    c. 26 pieces
    d. 162 pieces

32. ★ As you work your way through the exit of Toy Story Mania, look at the benches along the path. What game item are these benches made from?
    a. Blocks
    b. Playing cards
    c. Dice
    d. Dominoes

The Great Walt Disney World Scavenger Hunt

Alien Swirling Saucers

33. ★ As you approach Alien Swirling Saucers, notice the two guards on each side of the entrance. What common item are their shields made from?
    a. Space ship
    b. Record album
    c. Pizza
    d. Donut

34. ★★ As you make your way through the space port, find the console marked Mission Brief. Which quadrant is shown on this panel?
    a. Alpha
    b. Gamma
    c. Delta
    d. Beta

35. ★★ On the Operation Delta side of this display, which of these is *not* one of the operations shown?
    a. Display courage
    b. Defeat Zurg
    c. Defy detection
    d. Destroy defenses

36. ★★ Near the Docking Control you will find two Bays. Which number is to the right side of the two bays?
    a. 1
    b. 13
    c. 113
    d. 31

37. ★ As you exit Alien Swirling Saucers, find the alien inside his spaceship within the planter. What color is this spaceship?
    a. Blue
    b. Yellow
    c. White
    d. Red

Did you know?

As you walk through the area near Alien Swirling Sauce, you will find a larger than life Buzz Lightyear. Take a moment to stop for a once in a lifetime picture with this iconic Pixar character.

38. ★★ Find the restrooms within Toy Story Land, nearby your will find a drinking fountain with a Scrabble tile resting above. Which letter is this Scrabble tile?
    a. W
    b. V
    c. X
    d. Z

39. ★ High above you will see the Restroom sign spelled out in Scrabble tiles. What point value is the letter M in this sign?
    a. 1
    b. 2
    c. 3
    d. 4

> **Did you know?**
>
> The signs outside the Boy and Girl restrooms are spelled out with wooden alphabet blocks.

40. ★ Nearby, you will find a box of Sugar Coated Lass-o's. What town does the large B stand for at the top of the box?
    a. Battle Court
    b. Battle Creek
    c. Brittle Creek
    d. Branson Creek

> **Did you know?**
>
> As you wander through Andy's backyard, look down at the ground. You will see large sneaker prints made by Andy while playing with his toys.

Woody's Lunch Box

41. ★ As you approach Andy's Lunch Box, you will find Andy's thermos holding up the lid. What instrument do you see Jessie playing on this thermos?
    a. Guitar
    b. Drum
    c. Flute
    d. Harmonica

The Great Walt Disney World Scavenger Hunt

42. ★★ Behind Andy's thermos, you will find a plastic soldier holding an animal cracker. Which animal does this soldier hold?
    a. Cat
    b. Horse
    c. Turtle
    d. Bunny

43. ★ As you place your order, look above at the menu board. What lunchbox item is the menu printed on?
    a. Juice box
    b. Cookie box
    c. Milk carton
    d. Cracker box

44. ★★★ As you look around Andy's Lunchbox, you will find several packages with the word Babybel written on them. What food item do these packages contain?
    a. Cookies
    b. Crackers
    c. Cheese
    d. Fruit

45. ★★ Nearby, you will find a box of Tinker Toys. How many items are held within this circular box?
    a. 105
    b. 102
    c. 25
    d. 501

46. ★★ As you read the Tinker Toys box, in which year were Tinker Toys released?
    a. 1931
    b. 1955
    c. 1971
    d. 1913

47. ★ As you continue exploring Toy Story Land, you will come across a Play Family Camper. What color is the boat sitting atop this classic child's toy?
    a. Green
    b. Yellow
    c. Blue
    d. Red

48. ★ Within the camper, you will find a little person toy. What type of hat does this toy have on his head?
    a. Baseball hat
    b. Cowboy hat
    c. Policeman's hat
    d. Fireman's hat

49. ★★ On the path to Slinky Dog Dash, you will find several pencils standing on end. Which brand of pencil do you see?
    a. Cretacolor
    b. Faber-Castell
    c. Ticonderoga
    d. Pixar

Slinky Dog Dash

50. ★★★ As you approach the entrance to Slinky Dog Dash, notice the dog collar above with the wait time. What is the name of the Dog this collar belongs to?
    a. Buttercup
    b. Buster
    c. Scud
    d. Rex

51. ★★ As you work your way through the queue, you will come to the package for Slinky Dog. What is the name of the company that manufactures this toy?
    a. Pixar Industries
    b. Disney Industries
    c. James Industries
    d. Lasseter Industries

52. ★★ Find the instructions for Slinky Dog Dash. How many pieces come with this play set?
    a. 245
    b. 542
    c. 452
    d. 425

53. ★★ In what town does the manufacturing for Slinky Dog Coaster take place?
    a. Anaheim, Ca.
    b. Orlando, Fl.
    c. Marceline, Mo.
    d. Emeryville, Ca.

54. ★★★ Above your head, you will find a game board with X's and O's. What is the name of this child's game?
    a. Toss Across
    b. Connect Four
    c. Tic Tac Toe
    d. Mouse Trap

The Great Walt Disney World Scavenger Hunt

55. ★ Find the bath toy carton, what is the name of the Toy Story character that adorns the cover of this box?
    a. Squeaky
    b. Wheezy
    c. Dusty
    d. Squeezy

56. ★★ As you watch the safety video for Slinky Dog Dash, what sort of toy is this video being shown on?
    a. Etch A Sketch
    b. Leap Pad
    c. Camera
    d. View master

57. ★★★ As you enter Slinky Dog and begin your ride, you will find a box for Rex the dinosaur. What is the price of this toy from Al's Toy Barn?
    a. $19.99
    b. $9.95
    c. $19.95
    d. $9.99

Did you know?

Listen very carefully as Slinky rides along the track, you will hear his spring coil and uncoil as you go along your way.

---

58. ★★ As you reach the Big Finale, you will find Wheezy, Mr. Spell and Andy's tape recorder waiting for you. What toy does Andy's tape recorder rest on top of to your left?
    a. Pick up Sticks
    b. Pick up Straws
    c. Pick up your Room
    d. Pick up Snakes

Bonus question:

59. ★★★ What famous crooner is the voice of Wheezy when he sings *You've Got a Friend in Me*?
    a. Robert Goulet
    b. Bing Crosby
    c. Frank Sinatra
    d. Sammy Davis Jr.

60. ★★★ As you exit Slinky Dog Dash, you will find a book entitled *Mr. Picklepants Songs for Singing*. Which of these

is not one of the songs listed on the back cover of this book?

a.   *Herr Hedgehog*
b.   *Yodelay-he-Who?*
c.   *Alpining for You*
d.   *The Alpine Bounce*

Did you know?

Before your time in Toy Story Land ends, be sure to find the Green Army Men and watch their performance throughout Andy's Backyard.

Did you know?

Be sure to get your picture with the famous Luxo Ball you will find near Toy Story Mania,

Animation Courtyard

Go back to the beginnings of the Disney animation dynasty and discover the origins of founder Walt Disney in Animation Courtyard. Visit with some of your favorite characters at Disney Junior Live on Stage or visit with your favorite Star Wars characters at Launch Bay.

Walt Disney Presents – Gallery and Exhibits

1. ★★★ In what town was Walt Disney born?
   a. Marceline, Mo.
   b. Orlando, Fl.
   c. Anaheim, Ca.
   d. San Francisco, Ca.

2. ★★ Find Walt's second grade desk. In what year did Walt travel back to his school?
   a. 1965
   b. 1936
   c. 1955
   d. 1956

3. ★★ In 1916, Walt Disney went to see a production that changed the direction of his life. What book does the actress in the photo hold?
   a. *Snow White and the Seven Dwarves*
   b. *Pinocchio*
   c. *Peter Pan*
   d. *Cinderella*

4. ★★ In 1915, Walt Disney talked about his hero, Abraham Lincoln. How did Walt Disney commemorate the birthday of Abraham Lincoln each year?
   a. Giving a history lesson
   b. Singing a song
   c. Reciting the Gettysburg Address
   d. Painting a picture of Abraham Lincoln

5. ★★ One of Walt's earliest jobs was to sell newspapers and what other item on the trains?
   a. Soda
   b. Candy
   c. Cartoons
   d. Mints

6. ★ Find the Alice comics on the wall. What is the title of the comic book that appears in color?
   a. *Alice's Tea Party*
   b. *Alice's Spooky Adventure*
   c. *Alice Saves the Day*
   d. *Alice's Friends in Wonderland*

7. ★★★ The Disney Silly Symphony *the Skeleton Dance* debuted in what year?
   a. 1923
   b. 1926
   c. 1992
   d. 1929

8. ★★★ Find Walt Disney's artist desk. On the desk is a bottle of blue ink, what is the brand of this ink?
   a. Epson
   b. Sailor
   c. Carter's
   d. Iron Gull

9. ★★ In the Silly Symphony cartoon *the Band Concert*, what new character outshines the others?
   a. Donald Duck
   b. Goofy
   c. Pluto
   d. Oswald the Lucky Rabbit

The Great Walt Disney World Scavenger Hunt

10. ★★ As you look on Walt Disney's studio desk behind the glass, find the small plaque. Which actress gave Walt the Oscar at the Academy Awards?
    a. Audrey Hepburn
    b. Julie Andrews
    c. Annette Funicello
    d. Shirley Temple

11. ★★★ As you continue your exploration of the museum, you will find several shelves with toys inspired by Disney films. What is the name of the kitten seen with *Pinocchio*?
    a. Cleo
    b. Figaro
    c. Lampwick
    d. Gideon

12. ★★ In what cartoon did Donald Duck make his debut in 1934?
    a. *The Band Concert*
    b. *Moving Day*
    c. *The Wise Little Hen*
    d. *Orphan's Benefit*

Bonus question:

13. ★★★ Find the Dancing Man display, what famous actor was used for the dancing in this short film?
    a. Ray Bolger
    b. Gene Kelly
    c. Fred Astaire
    d. Buddy Ebsen

14. ★★ On what day in 1950 did Walt Disney make his network television debut?
    a. Christmas day
    b. Thanksgiving Day
    c. Easter Sunday
    d. Black Friday

15. ★★★ Stop for a moment in front of the television sets and watch the opening of Disneyland video. What famous song plays as the video begins?
    a. *It's a Small World*
    b. *Once Upon a Dream*
    c. *When you Wish Upon a Star*
    d. *The Unbirthday Song*

16. ★ Which Disney character helps your narrator show you the wonders of Disneyland?
    a. Mickey Mouse
    b. Tinker Bell
    c. Snow White
    d. Dopey

17. ★★ As you find the display for The Mickey Mouse Club, which of these names is *not* one of the original Mouseketeers?
    a. Dodie
    b. Cubbie
    c. Darlene
    d. Annette

18. ★★ Find the original artwork for Disneyland, how many acres were there for the park originally?
    a. 52 acres
    b. 45 acres
    c. 12 acres
    d. 42 acres

19. ★ Look high above your head, which beloved Disney character do you see flying above you?
    a. Dumbo
    b. Mary Poppins
    c. Peter Pan
    d. Tinker Bell

Did you know?

Betty Taylor wore the costume for Slue Foot Sue you see on display. Betty performed along with Wally Boag in the Golden Horseshoe at Disneyland resort. Betty and Wally died within one day of each other in 2011.

20. ★ As you find the animatronic for Abraham Lincoln, he was debuted at the 1964/65 world fair in which city?
    a. St. Louis
    b. New York
    c. Paris
    d. Vancouver

21. ★★ In what year did Disneyland Tokyo open?
    a. 1977
    b. 1980
    c. 1983
    d. 1993

The Great Walt Disney World Scavenger Hunt

22. ★ Find the model for The Tree of Life at the Animal Kingdom. How many hand carved animals can be found on this tree?
    a. 304
    b. 221
    c. 403
    d. 325

Did you know?

Throughout the year, this building houses special character meet and greets, as well as special sneak previews of new and exciting Disney films.

Walt Disney: One Man's Dream

23. ★★★ As you enter the theater and the film begins, why did Walt's dad sell the farm in Kansas?
    a. Couldn't make crops grow
    b. Wanted to become a newspaper man
    c. Illness
    d. Crops failed

24. ★★ After Walt failed as a cartoonist, he packed his belongings in what kind of suitcase?
    a. Cardboard
    b. Leather
    c. Canvas
    d. Burlap

25. ★★ How much money did Walt have in his pocket when he arrived in Hollywood?
    a. $30.00
    b. $40.00
    c. $50.00
    d. $20.00

26. ★★ What happened to Walt on the train ride from Manhattan to Los Angeles?
    a. He met his wife Lillian
    b. He created Snow White
    c. He met his brother Roy
    d. He created Mickey Mouse

27. ★ Who originally did the voice of Mickey Mouse?
    a. Roy Disney
    b. Jim Henson
    c. Spanky McFarland
    d. Walt Disney

28. ★★ In what year did Walt take Lillian on their first vacation ever?
    a. 1931
    b. 1951
    c. 1955
    d. 1966

29. ★ Where did they hold the premier of *Snow White and the Seven Dwarves* in 1937?
    a. Grauman's Chinese Theater
    b. Hyperion Theater
    c. Carthay Circle Theater
    d. Disneyland

Bonus Question

30. ★★★ What is the name of the film you see where the man is flying in his car with his dog?
    a. *The Shaggy Dog*
    b. *The Absent-Minded Professor*
    c. *Son of Flubber*
    d. *The Computer Wore Tennis Shoes*

Bonus Question

31. ★★★ Names the film you see with the twin girls singing on the stage?
    a. *Old Yeller*
    b. *Double Trouble*
    c. *Let's Get Together*
    d. *The Parent Trap*

32. ★★ Daddy daughter day was the beginning of what dream for Walt Disney?
    a. Walt Disney World
    b. Mary Poppins
    c. Disneyland
    d. The Disneyland Railroad

33. ★★ What famous Disney song do you hear as the film ends?
    a. *When You Wish Upon a Star*
    b. *World of Color*
    c. *I've Got No Strings*
    d. *Fantasmic*

34. ★★ What famous actress narrates Walt, One Man's Dream?
    a. Haley Mills
    b. Julie Andrews
    c. Angela Lansbury
    d. Doris Day

Did you know?

Throughout Animation Courtyard, you will find shows and events to relax during your day. Be sure to visit with The Voyage of the Little Mermaid or Disney Junior while visiting Animation Courtyard.

The Voyage of the Little Mermaid

35. ★★ As you wait for the theater to open, look around at the artifacts around the waiting area. Find the candlestick from Pinocchio, what character from the Disney classic was this candlestick found inside?
    a. Cleo
    b. Figaro
    c. Lampwick
    d. Monstro

36. ★★ What famous writer owned the fishing pole you see hanging on the wall?
    a. Wilde
    b. Hemmingway
    c. Twain
    d. Poe

37. ★★★ What famous book was written on the typewriter covered in minerals in the corner of this room?
    a. *The Old Man and the Sea*
    b. *Moby Dick*
    c. *20,000 League Under the Sea*
    d. *The Little Mermaid*

38. ★★ Find a worn lantern on one of the shelves. What literary character was imprisoned within this lantern?
    a. Tom Thumb
    b. Sebastien
    c. Tinkerbell
    d. Pinocchio

Disney's Animal Kingdom

Introduction

Disney's Animal Kingdom, the last and largest of the Walt Disney World major theme parks, began construction in 1990, immediately after the opening of Disney's Hollywood Studios. Disney's Animal Kingdom focuses on animal conservation, as well as bringing exotic animal to the guests of Walt Disney World resort.

Your journey begins at the Tree of Life where every animal is given sanctuary under its branches. Stand in the splendor of this man-made marvel as you search out the animals carved into its trunk.

As you travel through the vast jungles of Asia, Africa and Pandora, keep a sharp eye out for the strange an unusual. Every species from tigers to bats can be found on your journey. Surely, you will find your favorite wild creature as you stroll through the tree covered pathways.

Excitement comes to you as you ride over the top of Mount Everest and travel back in time to see dinosaurs long since extinct.

Discovery Island

Walk the quiet travels of Discovery Island to see creatures great and small before coming to a magnificent clearing where the Tree of Life stands in all her majesty over Disney's Animal Kingdom. Follow the tree of life roots down to become the size of a bug and don your honorary bug eyes in It's Tough to be a Bug.

Did you know?

Before you enter the park, stop and look at the parking sign. You will see a dragon amongst the other animals. There is a reason for this, Disney was planning a magical land where the dragon would be featured but the plan was rethought before the park opening. This dragon is all that remains.

1. ★ As you approach the front gates of the Animal Kingdom, what majestic animal do you see between Disney and Animal on the sign above the ticket booths?
   a. Lion
   b. Tiger
   c. Elephant
   d. Parrot

> ### Did you know?
> As you begin your journey into Disney's Animal Kingdom, keep an eye out for what appears to be a group of vines growing upright along the path. This wonderful camouflage is one of the Disney performers DiVine. Watch her come to life and dance in a mesmerizing performance.

> ### Did you know?
> As you get your first glimpse of The Tree of Life, marvel at this feat of engineering. The core is actually a refitted oil rig that the tree was created around.

It's Tough to be a Bug

2. ★★★ As you begin your decent under the Tree of Life, you will walk through a hollow log. Look above you, what species of Dinosaur do you see?
   a. Tyrannosaurus Rex c. Stegosaurus
   b. Dilophsaurus   d. Pterodactyl

> ### Did you know?
> All of the animals you see in the roots of the tree were hand carved by artists into the cement while it was still wet. The artist only had a certain amount of time before the concrete became too hard to work with.

3. ★★ On your journey, you will pass by several posters for the acts in It's Tough to be a Bug. On the Weevil Kneevil poster, what is the name of the newspaper for review at the bottom?

	a.	The Walnut Times	c.	The Hazelnut Register
	b.	The Acorn Street Journal	d.	The Almond Times

4. ★★ Which bug is featured on the poster for Claire De Room?
   a. Stink bug
   b. Dung beetle
   c. House fly
   d. Smell bug

5. ★ What sort of spider is featured on the poster for Chili?
   a. Black Widow
   b. Tarantula
   c. Brown Recluse
   d. Brazilian wandering spider

6. ★ As you get closer to the theater, you will find the theater posters for hit shows. What hit song is featured in *The Dung and I*?
   a. *Forever Dung*
   b. *We are Dung*
   c. *Hello Dung Lovers*
   d. *When We Were Dung*

7. ★★ As you read the poster for *Beauty and the Bees*, how many times a minute can bees beat their wings?
   a. 26,000
   b. 36,000
   c. 26,000,000
   d. 26

8. ★★ As you read the poster for *Antie*, Ants use their antenna to feel and what?
   a. Taste
   b. Talk
   c. Smell
   d. Hear

9. ★★ According to the poster for *Beauty and the Bees*, how much honey is produced from 60,000 flowers?
   a. One-quart
   b. One-pint
   c. One teaspoon
   d. One cup

10. ★★ According to the poster for *A Cockroach Line*, Cockroaches are what kind of eaters?

a.	Voracious	c.	Constant
b.	Picky	d.	Vegetable

11. ★ As you read the poster for *Web Side Story*, which type of spiders appear on the sign?
    - a. Black widow
    - b. Tarantula
    - c. Daddy Long Legs
    - d. Wolf Spider

12. ★★ As you read the poster for *Web Side Story*, how many times stronger is Black Widow venom than rattlesnake venom?
    - a. 10
    - b. 20
    - c. 25
    - d. 15

13. ★★ Find the poster for *Barefoot in the Bark*. According to this poster, how high do the African termite mounds get?
    - a. 30 feet
    - b. 40 feet
    - c. 50 feet
    - d. 45 feet

14. ★★ According to the poster for *Barefoot in the Bark*, how many termites can inhabit a single colony?
    - a. 2 million
    - b. 3 million
    - c. 4 million
    - d. 5 million

Did you know?

If you look toward the rear of the queue for the theater, you will find a large ball of dung suspended from the ceiling. This dung ball was created by imagineers to give you a feeling for being a bug yourself.

---

15. ★★ As you read the poster for *The Grass Menagerie*, what does the sign read that the bug holds up?
    - a. Help me
    - b. Hello there
    - c. Surprise
    - d. Hi mom

16. ★★ According to *The Grass Menagerie* poster, how many species of insects are there in the world?
    a. 8,000,000
    b. 80,000
    c. 180,000
    d. 800,000

17. ★★ If you read the poster for *My Fair Ladybug*, what type of animal are ladybugs?
    a. Bugs
    b. Beetles
    c. Aphids
    d. Insects

18. ★★★ As you take your seat in the theater and your show begins, the narrator requests you do not perform certain activities. Which of these is *not* one of the items listed?
    a. Jumping
    b. Pollinating
    c. Stinging
    d. Buzzing

19. ★ As the show begins, you will see Flik from *A Bug's Life* enter the theater. According to Flik, how long have bugs been doing their act?
    a. 30 million years
    b. 300 million years
    c. 3 million years
    d. 300 years

20. ★ As you watch the tarantula doing his act, what is his name?
    a. Chewy
    b. Changa
    c. Chili
    d. Willy

21. ★★ What does the tarantula use for targets during his portion of the show?
    a. Bugs
    b. Flowers
    c. Seeds
    d. Acorns

22. ★ What famous tagline does the soldier termite use when he leaves the stage?
    a. What you talkin' about
    b. I'll be back
    c. Adrienne!
    d. Yippee!

23. ★★ What does Flik tell the stink bug to lay off?
    a. Churros
    b. Cotton candy
    c. Pretzels
    d. Ice cream

24. ★★ As Hopper takes over the show, he shows video of several bug films. Which of these is *not* one of the attacking insects?
    a. Grasshoppers
    b. Ants
    c. Pill bugs
    d. Spiders

25. ★ What is the name on the can of bug spray Hopper used to attack you in your seats?
    a. Red Flag
    b. Bug Doom
    c. The Bug Zapper
    d. Exterminator

26. ★ What food item does the bug show you at the finale of It's Tough to be a Bug?
    a. Rotten cupcake
    b. Rotten churro
    c. Rotten candy bar
    d. Rotten carrot

27. ★★ At the end of the show, your narrator asks you to stay seated until the rest of the bugs exit the theater. Which of these is *not* one of the bugs mentioned?
    a. Maggots
    b. Beetles
    c. Cockroaches
    d. Grasshoppers

Africa

Travel through the quiet village of Harambe, which means come together, to visit with the locals. Stop and enjoy street performers as they show off their talents. Hop aboard an off-road vehicle to visit the animals of the savannah or take some time to stroll through the jungles to see gorilla or hippopotamus.

1. ★★★ As you enter the Africa section of Disney's Animal Kingdom, find the Tamu Tamu. On the corner are several notices, find the one for the hot air balloon rides, finish the line, "Longing for that _____ vision of Africa."
   a. Awesome   c. Romantic
   b. Dusty   d. Fascinating

2. ★★ As you continue reading the notices that are pasted to the building, what does Cap'N Bob's Super Safari's guarantee?
   a. Animals   c. Heat
   b. Bugs   d. Fun

3. ★★ Nearby, you will find the wooden sign for the Harambe Fort. In which year was it erected?

a.	1240	c.	1520
b.	1420	d.	1540

4. ★★ As you walk along the path you will find the Hotel Burudika. On the wooden door, what sort of alert is posted?
   a. Heat
   b. Insect
   c. Poaching
   d. Brush fire

5. ★★ Find the Mombasa Marketplace on your travels. Above this market is a sign for what sort of office?
   a. Safari office
   b. Attorney office
   c. Post office
   d. Survey office

Kilimanjaro Safaris

6. ★★★ As you approach the Kilimanjaro Safari attraction you will see a large tree above the entrance, what sort of tree is this?
   a. Quiver tree
   b. Baobab tree
   c. Marula tree
   d. Dragon Blood tree

7. ★ As you enter the queue for Kilimanjaro Safari, notice the signs above you. What is the African word for elephant?
   a. Tembo
   b. Twiga
   c. Simba
   d. Elephant

8. ★ What does the word Punda Milia translate to in English?
   a. Lion
   b. Beetles
   c. Zebra
   d. Alligator

9. ★ You will see live animals along your way to the safari, what is the name of the crane you see?
   a. Crowned crane
   b. Mohawk crane
   c. Peacock crane
   d. Tiara crane

The Great Walt Disney World Scavenger Hunt

10. ★ As you enter the safari booking office, what sort of animal adorns the thermometer to your right?
    a. Cheetah
    b. Hippo
    c. Giraffe
    d. Lion

11. ★★ As you enter the safari booking office, you will see a dollar framed above the desk. What denomination is the framed bill?
    a. 20 dollars
    b. 2 pounds
    c. 10 pounds
    d. 20 pounds

12. ★ Continue reading the signs along the path. How many hours a day do lions sleep?
    a. 24 hours
    b. 20 hours
    c. 15 hours
    d. 25 hours

Did you know?

A full-grown hippopotamus can outrun a human on land.

---

13. ★ As you enter your safari vehicle and your guide begins your tour, he will say "Jambo" to you. What does this mean?
    a. Welcome
    b. Good luck
    c. Hello
    d. Warning

14. ★★ What animal are the Okapi relatives of according to your guide?
    a. Giraffe
    b. Zebra
    c. Elephant
    d. Cheetah

15. ★★ As you come to the Bongo enclosure, what are they known as in the jungle?
    a. Clowns
    b. Animals
    c. Ghosts
    d. Kings

16. ⭐ How long can Hippopotamus hold their breath underwater?
    a. 6 minutes
    b. 15 minutes
    c. 10 minutes
    d. 8 minutes

17. ⭐⭐ What species of crocodile do you see below as the safari passes over the bridge?
    a. New Guinea crocodile
    b. Nile crocodile
    c. Slender snouted crocodile
    d. Mugger crocodile

18. ⭐⭐ How do the crocodiles protect their young when the think they are in danger?
    a. Charge the attacker
    b. Sit on top of them
    c. Hide them in the trees
    d. Put them in their mouth

19. ⭐⭐ Why do the elephants eat the red clay from the red clay pits?
    a. Helps digest their food
    b. To cool off
    c. It tastes good
    d. Good for their skin

20. ⭐⭐ What are the largest birds in the world according to your guide?
    a. Vultures
    b. Pelican
    c. Ostrich
    d. Emu

21. ⭐⭐ What is the male lion's job in the pride?
    a. Hunting
    b. Protect the pride
    c. Lay around and sleep
    d. Take care of the young

The Great Walt Disney World Scavenger Hunt

Gorilla Falls Exploration Trail

22. ★★ As you enter the Gorilla Falls Exploration Trail, you will find a small cart with a yellow license plate. Which is the correct number on this license plate?
    a. WED1977
    b. UZ1172
    c. ZU2298
    d. GF2222

23. ★ Find the welcome sign for the Pangani Forest Conservation School. Finish this quote, "We do not inherit the earth from our parents – we borrow it from _____."
    a. The future
    b. The earth
    c. From future generations
    d. Our children

24. ★★ Stop for a moment to read the posting of instructions within the wildlife reserve. What are you advised not to do that would disrupt the animal's natural behavior?
    a. Make excessive noise
    b. Fire guns
    c. Feed them
    d. Take them home

25. ★★ According to this notice, who has the right of way?
    a. The park rangers
    b. The animals
    c. The humans
    d. The off-road vehicles

26. ★ Find the Colobus Monkey. Which of these are *not* one of the items in their diet according to the postings?
    a. Buds
    b. Leaves
    c. Fruit
    d. Thistles

27. ★★★ Along the trail you will find two wooden crates with addresses on them. The smaller of the two is addressed to which famous wildlife pioneer?
    a. Jane Goodall
    b. Donald Watson
    c. Jerry Vlasak
    d. Jane Doe

28. ★★ Enter the Research Center building and find the research notes with gorilla drawings. What does the gorilla construct within ten minutes according to the notes?
    a. His meal
    b. A hut
    c. A nest
    d. A bath

29. ★★★ Find and read the letter from Debra Peterson. According to the letter, how many gorillas are left in the wild?
    a. 2,000
    b. 5,000
    c. 10,000
    d. 500

30. ★★★ As you read the notices around this building, what animal is causing destruction of the native fresh water fish population?
    a. Nile perch
    b. Nile crocodile
    c. Nile frog
    d. Nile bats

Pandora – The World of Avatar

Enter the futuristic world of Pandora and explore the world of Avatar like never before. Examine the beauty of bioluminescent plant life or stand in awe at the floating mountains towering high above you. For the bravest of warriors, fly on a mountain Banshee or, for those looking for lesser thrills, take a leisurely ride down the Na'Vi river.

Did you know?

As you enter Pandora, you will notice a large plant known in Avatar as Flaska Reclinata. Touch this plant and you will feel a cool mist showering down upon you.

Did you know?

As you journey through Pandora, listen to the sounds of this jungle. If you visit at different times throughout the day and evening, notice the sounds of the creature's change as if some are resting while others are coming to life around you.

> ### Did you know?
> Find the drum circle where children of all ages can strike the drums to hear the sounds of Pandora. Be aware of where the sounds are coming from as you may just hear the drum echoing from overhead instead of from the drum beneath your hand.

1. ✯ As you enter Pandora, stop and read the visitor information sign. What do the words "Oel Ngati Kameie" mean?
    a. I need you
    b. I see you
    c. I love you
    d. I fear you

2. ✯ According to the visitor information, what are you advised to do if you encounter a large animal?
    a. Do not run
    b. Runaway
    c. Scream
    d. Fall to the ground

> ### Did you know?
> As you walk through Pandora, enjoy the immense beauty around you. At night, the jungle comes alive with bioluminescence for an enhanced experience.

3. ✯✯ As you approach the queue for Flights of Passage, notice a large pond with a warning sign opposite this attraction. According to warning sign, sudden arm movement will trigger what response from the creatures?
    a. Spitting
    b. Screaming
    c. Jumping
    d. Hunting

The Great Walt Disney World Scavenger Hunt

Na'Vi River Journey

> **Did you know?**
>
> Before entering the queue for the Na'Vi River Journey, look down at the ground. You will notice the large footprints of the Na'Vi embedded in the ground. Notice there are child footprints included in this feature.

> **Did you know?**
>
> As you float down the river, look up at the large leaves, you will see creatures hopping from leaf to leaf from above.

> **Did you know?**
>
> As you approach the shaman, sitting at the river edge, this is the most advanced animatronic figure Disney has developed to date.

Avatar Flight of Passage

4. ★★★ As you walk up the path of Avatar Flights of Passage, stop of a moment just before entering the cave. High above you will see some very small creatures sleeping in the carved rock of the floating mountains. What is the name of these creatures?
   a. Sap bats
   b. Stink bats
   c. Sting bats
   d. Sting birds

> ### Did you know?
> As you approach the cave for Flights of Passage, you will see a waterfall very high above on the side of the cliff. If you look very carefully, you will notice this is not actually a waterfall but a rotating wheel that gives the appearance of water complete with mesh netting to appear like mist from the falling water.

> ### Did you know?
> As you enter the cave, look around at the drawings left behind by the Na'Vi. The enormous blue bird like creature is a nod to the wonders you are about to experience for yourself.

5. ★★ You will come to the first airlock door as you work your way through the queue. As you examine the operation procedure, number three does what?
    a. Wait for door release
    b. Prep rebreather
    c. Activate at 90%
    d. Select (hostile) ATMO

6. ★★ As you enter the remains of the RDA operation, stop to read the Mountain Banshee Project sign. What is the purpose of this project?
    a. Reverse habitat destruction
    b. Offer healthcare to Banshee
    c. Re-establishing food sources
    d. Cleaning the water

The Great Walt Disney World Scavenger Hunt

Bonus question:

7. ★★★ Find the corrugated metal with the JC shoring logo. On this metal is the number 08.16.54, what is the meaning of this number?
   a. Movie release date
   b. James Cameron's birthday
   c. The day RDA arrived on Pandora
   d. Sigourney Weavers birthday

8. ★★ According to the corrugated metal left behind, what is the Tensile held strength?
   a. 4,000 PSI
   b. 40,000 PSI
   c. 10,000 PSI
   d. 3,624 pounds

9. ★★★ High above your head, find the bright yellow strut. According to the warning label, what are struts not to be used as in trenching operations?
   a. A shovel
   b. A bucket
   c. A ladder
   d. A hose

10. ★★ Find the biohazard Level 3 chart. According to the chart, what was the last check in time for BC?
    a. 18:32
    b. 7:13
    c. 10:16
    d. 16:10

11. ★★ Look closely to find the Failure to Report warning in the area of the chart. What specifically does this sign address?
    a. Injuries
    b. Illness
    c. Treasure
    d. New discoveries

12. ★★ Find the RDA toxic systems inspection guideline sign. The standard testing kit is used for how many minutes?
    a. Ten minutes
    b. Two minutes
    c. Twenty-two minutes
    d. Twenty minutes

13. ★★ As you work your way through the remains of the RDA site, find the four colored pipes above your head. What does the red pipe contain?
    a. Nitrogen
    b. Suppression agent
    c. Portable water
    d. Compressed ATMO

> ### Did you know?
> Just before entering the lab portion of the queue, look down below the queue, you will find a large black pit with discarded bottles nearby. Even though the jungle has overtaken the RDA facility, the remains of humans are all around you.

14. ★★★ As you enter the lab, you will pass by a large gray door. In what year w/as this door manufactured?
    a. 1998
    b. 2001
    c. 2101
    d. 2805

15. ★ Find the Threats to the Banshee Ecosystem chart. What species of Banshee is featured on this poster?
    a. Goldstone
    b. Keystone
    c. Brownstone
    d. Blackstone

16. ★★ As you follow the chart, what kind of wasp will have a population explosion if the fan lizard population collapses?
    a. Hellfire
    b. Bonfire
    c. Wildfire
    d. Icefire

17. ★★★ Where do Fan lizards create their nests according to the Banshee Ecosystem Chart?
    a. Swamps
    b. Rocks
    c. Trees
    d. Floating mountains

The Great Walt Disney World Scavenger Hunt

18. ★★ As you circle the lab, look in the center area. Find the book *Water Treatment book* by Elsevier. What emerging technology is this book about?
    a. Nanofabrication
    b. Robot
    c. Desalinization
    d. Membrane

19. ★★ As you pass by the small cages, watch the creatures within move. According to the notes, more dirt equals what?
    a. Angry creatures
    b. More food
    c. More waste
    d. More activity

Did you know?

Find the book entitled *Pandoran Botany* in the lab area. The author, Dr. Grace Augustine was played by Sigourney Weaver in the film *Avatar* and literally wrote the book on Pandora botany. This book is a small nod to the character from the famous film.

---

20. ★★★ Within the lab, you will find a three-ring binder open with a small sticky note attached. What are they waiting for to continue further testing according to the note?
    a. Supplies
    b. Samples
    c. Environment
    d. Animals

21. ★★★ Find the open notebook with the yellow reminder note at the top. At XX 24, what was the response to extreme heat according to these notes?
    a. Died from the heat
    b. Multiplied
    c. Embraced the flames
    d. Remained still

22. ★★ You will come across another book written by Dr Ogden featuring her picture on the front cover. What is the correct title of this book?
    a. *ACORN My Connection*
    b. *IKRAN My Connection*
    c. *IKRAN My Convulsion*
    d. *IRAN My connection*

23. ★★★ Find the clipboard with the kitty cat sticky notes on the front. What takes a long time to replace according to the note?
    a. Earth equipment
    b. Rocket fuel
    c. Earth food
    d. Lab assistants

24. ★★★ Find the bulletin board with the drawings and notices, what is missing according to the note from Abe?
    a. Rock samples
    b. Plant samples
    c. Rock sample castings
    d. Decommissioned bug screen

25. ★★ What item has finally arrived according to the note to team banshee?
    a. T shirts
    b. Baseballs caps
    c. Keychains
    d. Coffee mugs

26. ★★ Find the notice for Team Banshee practice. What sort of sport are they playing on Pandora?
    a. Softball
    b. Baseball
    c. Football
    d. Soccer

Did you know?

As you exit the lab, you will find yourself in a large room with a banshee mural on one wall. If you look at the signs for the Utilidors, notice a basketball sign. Apparently, the technicians have a basketball court.

The Great Walt Disney World Scavenger Hunt

27. ★ Which of these facilities is not housed on Utilidor level 4?
    a. Hvac diffuser
    b. Medical
    c. Electric power mains
    d. Atmo supply

28. ★★ As you enter the final stage before travelling on your banshee, what are you being scanned for?
    a. Diseases
    b. smuggled items
    c. Parasites
    d. Weapons

29. ★★★ Watch as the different creatures flash across the screen. How prevalent is the Manducus Taurus on Pandora?
    a. Common
    b. Rare
    c. Extinct
    d. Endangered

30. ★★ Who is credited with developing the technology to link your DNA with Na'Vi?
    a. James Cameron
    b. Dr. Weaver
    c. Dr. Goodall
    d. Dr. Ogden

Did you know?

As you watch the genetic matching system, move around and you will notice your picture on the screen moves with you.

Did you know?

As you exit Avatar Flights of Passage, you may notice three human hand prints with initials on an unassuming concrete wall. Included with the producers of Avatar is the director's handprint, James Cameron.

Asia

Enter the fictional area of Anandapur to indulge in the sights and sounds of Asia. Towering high above is the newest peak in the Disney mountain range, Expedition Everest. Beware of the Yeti that resides on this mystical mountain. Ride along the Kali river but beware of the rapids where you will undoubtedly get soaked before your trip is over.

1. ★★ As you enter the Asia area and walk along the path, stop for a moment at the large grouping of signs. What sort of cliffs are just up ahead?
    a. Mountain goat cliffs
    c. Bat cliffs
    b. Road runner cliffs
    d. Rat cliffs

2. ★★ What is the festival advertised on the green sign?
    a. Mountain festival
    c. Bat festival
    b. Yeti festival
    d. Lantern festival

3. ★ Find the sign for the Yeti Palace Hotel painted on the nearby building. When does this hotel open?
    a. Next season
    c. Next month
    b. Next year
    d. Next week

4. ★★ Along the path is a set of notices with a wire frame around them. Find the notice for the "Yeti is Real". What day of the week does this seminar meet?
   a. Wednesday
   b. Saturday
   c. Tuesday
   d. Monday

5. ★★★ Find the set of three wheels painted red with gold markings. What is the purpose of these wheels?
   a. Water pump
   b. Prayer
   c. Warning
   d. Magic

6. ★★ Find the blue sign for the Café Chital. Which of these is *not* one of the cuisines they offer?
   a. Mexican
   b. British
   c. Mandarin
   d. French

Maharaja Jungle Trek

7. ★★ As you enter the Maharaja Jungle Trek, read the history of this area. In what year was it decreed a preserve?
   a. 1544
   b. 1948
   c. 1454
   d. 1448

8. ★ As you approach the bat enclosure, according to the visitor advisement you should act quiet and what?
   a. Courteous
   b. Respectful
   c. Noisy
   d. Afraid

9. ★★★ As you approach the tiger enclosure, stop for a moment to read about the habitat. What percent of the tiger habitat remains in the wild?
   a. 100%
   b. 50%
   c. 20%
   d. 7%

10. ★★★ Read the letter from the wilderness explorers. Why are the tigers losing their habitat?
    a. Taken to zoos
    b. Not enough food
    c. Deforestation
    d. Migration

Did you know?

If you look at the return address on the envelope from the Wilderness Explorers the city is Emeryville, Ca. This is the headquarters for Pixar, the company that created the film Up in which Russell is a Wilderness Explorer.

---

11. ★★ Find the small sign with the blue writing for safe drinking water. According to the sign, which of these types of water is not included on the sign?
    a. Local water
    b. River water
    c. Standing water
    d. Water from unidentified sources

12. ★★ Along the path towards Expedition Everest you will find a small building with souvenirs. Outside you will find a sign that reads, "No strollers, carts, motorized scooters or _____." Finish the sign.
    a. Children
    b. Food
    c. Livestock
    d. Money

13. ★★ As you continue your travels you will come across a currency chart. What is the currency of South Africa according to the chart?
    a. Dollar
    b. Rand
    c. Euro
    d. Franc

The Great Walt Disney World Scavenger Hunt

Expedition Everest – Legend of the Forbidden Mountain

14. ★★ As you approach the entrance of Expedition Everest you will see a large rock with several warning signs. Which of these is *not* one of the descriptions of the travelers being warned?
    a. Climbers
    b. Travelers
    c. Trekkers
    d. Visitors

15. ★★ Find the sign to measure the height for riders. You must be as tall as what to ride?
    a. Mickey Mouse
    b. One Yeti foot
    c. A baby Yeti
    d. Donald Duck

16. ★★★ As you enter the first office, pause to read some of the signs and notices on the walls. How many horses are needed for the trek from Serka Zong to Mustang?
    a. Ten
    b. Twenty
    c. Seventeen
    d. Fifty-two

17. ★★ Read the board for the expeditions and tours behind the travel desk. What is the name on the VIP tour?
    a. Walt Disney
    b. Roy Disney
    c. Dan Casteel
    d. X Atencio

18. ★★ Take a look at the notes on the desk. What is written on the yellow post it note?
    a. Just keep climbing
    b. Long live the king
    c. The Yeti is real
    d. Stay centered

Did you know?

The Yeti is a creature known in Nepal folklore. Similar to Big Foot and the Abominable Snowman.

19. ★★ What is the legal weight limit per porter according to the sign in the office?
    a. 37 Pounds
    b. 73 Kilos
    c. 73 Pounds
    d. 37 Kilos

20. ★★ As you enter the Tashi's Trek, read the sign for proper clothing. Which of these is *not* one of the items listed on the sign?
    a. Water proof shell
    b. Glacier glasses
    c. Electric underwear
    d. Wool or fleece sweater

21. ★★★ Find the sign that reads "Respect the power of the Yeti. The Yeti is the guardian of what?
    a. The reclusive mountain
    b. The forbidden mountain
    c. The mountain creatures
    d. The snow mountain

22. ★ Enter Tashi's Trek shop and find the menu on the wall. How much does the Chapatis cost?
    a. 75
    b. 100
    c. 25
    d. 50

23. ★★★ As you look around the office, find the operating license for the Yeti museum. What is the certificate number on this license?
    a. 15930
    b. 51390
    c. 91530
    d. 19350

24. ★★ Read the plaques and newspaper articles around the room. What is the name of the curator of the Yeti Museum?
    a. Pema Djori
    b. Manghi Singh
    c. Yasri Tmana
    d. Mahatma Ghandi

The Great Walt Disney World Scavenger Hunt

25. ★ As you wander through the museum find the mural for Royal Anandapur. What product is this mural advertising?
    a. Coffee
    b. Bread
    c. Spices
    d. Tea

26. ★★ As you wind your way through the queue, notice the small blue sign asking to remove something before entering. What is it you must remove?
    a. Shoes
    b. Crampons
    c. Hat
    d. Clothing

Dinoland U.S.A.

Go back in time to the age of Dinosaurs when you walk through the gates of Dinoland U.S.A. Take an adventure to bring the dinosaur back to our time. Try your luck to win a prehistoric prize. Don't miss out on spinning madly on your very own dinosaur. Top off your time in Dinoland U.S.A. with a bite to eat, you will be glad you did.

1. ★★ As you pass through the gates of Dinoland U.S.A., stop for a moment and look at the logo for the Dino Institute. Which of these is *not* one of the words describing the Institute?
    a. Exploration
    b. Exultation
    c. Exhumation
    d. Excavation

2. ★★★ Find the Trilobites sign nearby. What species of dinosaur is seen on this sign?
    a. Sauropod
    b. Titanosaurus
    c. Velociraptor
    d. Pterodactyl

3. ★★ Find the Oldengate Bridge as you enter Dinoland U.S.A. As you read the brass plaque, how tall did the Brachiosaurus stand?
    a. 52 feet
    b. 25 inches
    c. 25 feet
    d. 52 inches

4. ★★ The original fossil for the Oldengate Bridge was found in Colorado in what year?
   a. 1955
   b. 1800
   c. 1977
   d. 1900

The Boneyard

5. ★ As you enter the Fossil Fun Site, look up at the sign. In what year was this established?
   a. 1974
   b. 1907
   c. 1947
   d. 1847

6. ★★★ Find the Track Ways sign as you explore the Bone Yard. Which researcher wrote the small note questioning the chase scene as invalid?
   a. Jenny
   b. Dr. Woo
   c. Jack Hammer
   d. Tom Ritz

7. ★★★ As you continue your discovery of the Fossil Fun Site, which species of dinosaur was excavated first in this area?
   a. Pterodactyl
   b. T Rex
   c. Velociraptor
   d. Brachiosaurus

8. ★★ On your travels through Dinoland U.S.A. you will come across a glass case with several notices within. What is the name of the museum director for the Dino Institute?
   a. Diana Sore
   b. Dinah Shore
   c. Abbey Normal
   d. Tina Stone

9. ★★ As you continue reading the notices, what did the Brachiosaurus lose?
   a. His head
   b. His spleen
   c. His tail
   d. His mind

10. ★★ What activity is going to take place on September 4 in the bone yard?
    a. Midnight dig
    b. Dino movie night
    c. Hide and seek in the bones
    d. Line dancing

11. ★★ What is Dr. Woo willing to trade for a sensible family car?
    a. 1952 Edsel
    b. 1915 Model T
    c. 1968 van
    d. 1983 Porsche

12. ★★★ What is the senior paleontologists favorite quote?
    a. I'm the greatest!
    b. Get to work!
    c. Dinosaurs rock!
    d. Time for work!

13. ★★ Finish this quote by Dr. Eugene McGee, "Every great advance in natural knowledge has involved the absolute _____ of authority?
    a. Rejection
    b. Questioning
    c. Abiding
    d. Following

14. ★★ Find the list of items in the lower corner of the box. What is the ninth item on this list?
    a. Leisure suit
    b. Rack of water pistols
    c. Keg spout
    d. Comparable brain

Did you know?

In the far-right box, you will find a hand drawn map. Look closely and you will see several of the attractions in and around Dinoland U.S.A. Be sure to stop to read the little quips about each item on the map.

The Great Walt Disney World Scavenger Hunt

15. ★ As you come to Chester and Hester's Dino-rama, you will find a billboard with several dinosaurs in a red convertible. How many Dinosaurs do you see?
    a. 7
    b. 8
    c. 4
    d. 5

> **Did you know?**
>
> Find the sign for Diggs County route 498. This cute sign is a homage to the opening date of Animal Kingdom at Walt Disney World April, 1998.

Primeval Whirl

16. ★ As you approach the Primeval Whirl attraction take a close look at the sign above you. What color is the kerchief the T rex is carrying?
    a. Green
    b. Blue
    c. Red
    d. Yellow

17. ★ On the sign for Primeval Whirl attraction, what is the smaller dinosaur saying about this ride?
    a. This really stinks
    b. Duck T rex duck
    c. Who said this is fun?
    d. This really extincts

> **Did you know?**
>
> The sign for Primeval Whirl has several meteors and dinosaurs running from them. This is a spoof on the long running theory that the dinosaurs were wiped from the face of the earth by a meteor that hit the earth during their time.

18. ★ As you walk through Dinoland USA you will find a billboard advertising the parking lot. How much is parking currently according to the sign?

a.	$ 2.00	c.	$20.00
b.	$ .50	d.	$50.00

> ### Did you know?
>
> If you look at the fence just below the sign for the parking lot it says "Sorry, lot full." This is an attempt by Animal Kingdom to keep guests from wandering backstage.

Chester and Hester's Dinosaur Treasures

19. ★ On the rooftop of Chester and Hester's you will find a sign that reads, "Going out of _____."
    a. This world
    b. Existence
    c. Business
    d. Our world

20. ★ On the sign that reads, "Prehistoric princes, mammoth deals." How many of the letters are yellow?
    a. 1
    b. 28
    c. 25
    d. 3

21. ★★ What product do the signs for rough scaly skin beneath the eaves of Chester and Hester's advertise?
    a. Burma scale
    b. Scale burn
    c. Fossil foam
    d. Fossil shave

22. ★★★ What year is stamped on the box holding up the small bones display?
    a. 1955
    b. 1953
    c. 1977
    d. 1453

23. ★★★ High above you find the road sign that reads, "_____ next 25 miles."
    a. Pteranodon
    b. Pterodactyl
    c. Dinosaurs
    d. Triceratops

24. ★★★ High above you, find the dinosaur drawn on the wall. What everyday item makes up the back and tail of this dinosaur?
    a. Rope
    b. Wood
    c. Measuring sticks
    d. Toothpicks

> **Did you know?**
>
> If you look among the décor above your head you will find a marionette of Mickey Mouse in his top hat and tails.

25. ★ Find the large green inflatable dinosaur in the center of the room. What does the sign around him read?
    a. Guard dino
    b. Party dino
    c. Number 1 dino
    d. Dino for sale

> **Did you know?**
>
> If you look high above your head at the ceiling of Chester and Hester's, you will find dinosaur footprints marching across the beams.

26. ★ Outside of Chester and Hester's you will find a Souvenir Photo area. You will find several license plates on the edge. Which of these is the correct number of the red plate on the corner of this small building?
    a. CBH794
    b. DO6207
    c. 12W6202
    d. LZS433

27. ★ Outside the souvenir photo area you will find two gas pumps. What is the cost of a gallon of gas on the pump to your left?
    a. $2.97
    b. $ .20 ½
    c. $1.20 9/10
    d. $ .50 9/10

28. ★ Find the Cretaceous Trail. How many years ago did this era of dinosaurs exist?
    a. 65 million
    c. 75 million
    b. 55 million
    d. 45 million

> **Did you know?**
>
> The replica of the Tyrannosaurus Rex you see along the path is the most complete fossil of a T Rex ever found. The original fossil has been instrumental in the study of these amazing animals.

29. ★ What is the name of the Tyrannosaurus Rex you see on the path towards the DINOSAUR! Attraction?
    a. Sue
    c. Rexxy
    b. Wanda
    d. T-bone

> **Did you know?**
>
> The Cretaceous Period is the last period where dinosaurs existed on earth.

DINOSAUR

30. ★★★ In what year was the Dino Institute dedicated?
    a. 1947
    c. 1978
    b. 1958
    d. 1977

> **Did you know?**
>
> Just before you walk through doors of the Dino Institute look to the wall opposite the doors. You will find a large T Rex head sticking out of the wall.

31. ★★ Find the plaque for the Albertosaurus. What region did this dinosaur live during the late cretaceous period?
    a. Europe
    b. Northern Africa
    c. Eastern North America
    d. Western North America

32. ★★ Which of these is not one of the theories of extinction on the mural in the Dino Institute?
    a. Egg eating mammals
    b. Worldwide flooding
    c. Disease
    d. Climate change

33. ★★ Find the plaque for the Carnotaurus. What sort of face does this dinosaur possess?
    a. Cat like
    b. Mouse like
    c. Bull dog like
    d. Bear like

Bonus question:

34. ★★★ As you watch the introduction video, what famous actress plays Dr. Marsh?
    a. Halle Barry
    b. Phylicia Rashad
    c. Angela Bassett
    d. Taraji P. Henson

35. ★ As the introduction video finish, your host states, "The future is truly _____?
    a. In the past
    b. At your fingertips
    c. An exciting adventure
    d. A wondrous place

36. ★★ As Dr. Seeker interrupts the presentation, what sort of scientist does he say he is?
    a. Geologist
    b. Physicist
    c. Neurobiologist
    d. Paleontologist

37. ★★ What period of time will you be visiting in the rover?
    a. Mesozoic
    b. Triassic
    c. Cretaceous
    d. Jurassic

38. ★★ What species of dinosaur does Dr. Seeker want you to bring back with you in the time rover?
    a. Albertosaurus
    b. Iguanodon
    c. Triceratops
    d. Kronosaurus

39. ★★ What activity interrupts the homing signal of the time rover according to Dr. Seeker?
    a. Gum chewing
    b. Exiting the vehicle
    c. Flash photography
    d. Interacting with the animal life

Did you know?

The ride Dinosaur is based on the film of the same name release by Disney in 2000. The film plot follows an abandoned iguanodon in his search for other dinosaurs while trying to survive predators.

40. ★★★ As you encounter several other species of dinosaurs, what sort of eating habit does the sauropod have?
    a. Carnivore
    b. Omnivore
    c. Planktivore
    d. Vegetarian

41. ★★★ As you go through your journey to the past, what sort of dinosaur is trying to eat you along the way?
    a. Carnotaurus
    b. Tyrannosaurus Rex
    c. Velociraptor
    d. Iguanodon

The Great Walt Disney World Scavenger Hunt

Dino-Bytes Snacks

42. ★ As you stand in front of Dino-bytes Snacks, find the dinosaurs standing on the rooftop. Which word on the small sign has been crossed out?
    a. Queen
    b. Dig
    c. Dinosaur
    d. King

Restaurantosaurus

43. ★ As you stand before Restaurantosaurus, notice the shiny silver motorhome in front of the building. Which of these is the correct number painting on the rear of the vehicle?
    a. 14255
    b. 15244
    c. 12544
    d. 21524

44. ★★ Look on the roof above you at the two blue chairs. What street sign do you see behind these chairs?
    a. Ped Xing
    b. Stop
    c. One-way
    d. No U turns

45. ★ Enter the building and find the notice board in the glass case. What special day is happening tomorrow according to the posting with the green dinosaur?
    a. Hawaiian shirt day
    b. Crazy hat day
    c. Pajama day
    d. Bring your pet to work day

46. ★★ What animated classic short will be playing at the double feature?
    a. *Plane Crazy*
    b. *Skeleton Dance*
    c. *Flowers and Trees*
    d. *Gertie the Dinosaur*

47. ★★★ Who is hosting a poker game at 7 pm?
    a. Animal
    b. Gertie
    c. Jenny
    d. Harold

48. ★★★ Read the intern notice from Dr. Bernard Dunn. He advises the interns to refrain from youthful exuberance and loud conduct after what hour?
    a. 1 am
    b. 11 pm
    c. 10 pm
    d. 3 am

49. ★★★ As you continue reading this notice he refers to what sort of party in the commissary?
    a. Soiree
    b. Shindig
    c. Bacchanal
    d. Hootenanny

50. ★★★ Continue reading the notices, in what city was the time rover unveiled by Dr. Helen Marsh to members of the scientific media?
    a. Orlando, Fl.
    b. Anaheim, Ca.
    c. Walla Walla, Wa.
    d. Bisby, Az.

51. ★★★ Dr. Marsh is known by what for turning cash poor operations into box-office bonanzas?
    a. Queen of the dinosaurs
    b. Midas of the museum world
    c. Empress of excavation site
    d. Divas of the digs

52. ★★★ Search the notices very closely. What is the zip code for Dinoland USA?
    a. 92802-2319
    b. 32830
    c. 55589-9054
    d. 90549-5558

53. ★★ As you explore the Restaurantosaurus, what is the phone number for Rex's Towing?
    a. 555-DINO
    b. 555-GERT
    c. 555-TREX
    d. 555-SEYA

54. ★★ Find the dinosaur on the wall in black ink. What part of the body makes up this artwork?
    a. Footprints
    b. Handprints
    c. Fingerprints
    d. Lip prints

As you finish your tour of the Walt Disney World resort, I hope you have seen the parks through new eyes. First time guests, my hope is to help you get the most out of your time. Frequent visitors, if you found even two new attractions to, I have succeeded in my mission.

My love of all things Disney continues daily knowing a new thrill is waiting for me next time I visit the parks. Never would I want to have a day when I did not find something new to fall in love with at the Walt Disney World resort.

Answer Key

Magic Kingdom

Esplanade

1. B – E
2. A – Yesterday

Main Street

Main Street Train Station

1. B – America's Forests
2. A – Ulysses Grant
3. B – Drum
4. D – Gloves
5. A – Messenger
6. C – Civilization
7. D – Ten cents
8. C – Big Boy
9. D – 1908
10. A - Engineman
11. D – 1871

Main Street Firehouse

12. A – 71
13. C – Blasting Powder
14. B – Shout
15. D – Horseshoe nails

Harmony Barber Shop

16. B - $25.00
17. A – Blue

Emporium

18. C – 66
19. D – A peddler
20. B – Take over the undersea kingdom
21. C – 1991
22. C - Wardrobe
23. A – Inspiration

Main Street Confectionary

24. D – Cloud
25. B – Chicago
26. C – Winnowing
27. B – Statue of Liberty

Casey's Corner

28. A – 15 cents
29. D – 2 runs
30. A – Butcher Boy Orton
31. C – Ear muffs

The Great Walt Disney World Scavenger Hunt

Hub

1. C - Parents

Fantasyland
Cinderella Castle

1. B – Mice turn into horses
2. C – Gus and Jack
3. D – Beads
4. A - Lucifer
5. A – Willie the giant

Castle Couture

6. D – Clariette

The Many Adventures of Winnie the Pooh

7. D – Mr. Sanders
8. A – Flyswatter
9. B – Blue
10. C – East
11. D – Red
12. B – 4
13. A – Tigger
14. D – 5
15. D – Red and white
16. C – A chair
17. B – Yawn
18. D – Christopher Robin

Mickey's PhilharMagic

19. A – A baton
20. B - 3

21. D - Hades
22. C – Final squeaks
23. A - Sleeping
24. B - Flute
25. A – So This is Love

Seven Dwarves Mine Train

26. A – Blue
27. B – Dopey
28. D – Skunk
29. C – 5:00

Mad Tea Party

30. C – Yellow

Storybook Circus

31. D – Monkey
32. B – Ridiculous

Pete's Silly Sideshow

33. A – Snort
34. C – 4
35. B – 5
36. D – Snake charmer
37. B – Clara Cluck
38. C – Unicycle

Casey Jr. Splash and Soak Station

39. A – Elephants
40. D – Spitting

The Barnstormer

41. C – Out flying
42. B – Smoke
43. A – Bowling ball

Dumbo the Flying Elephant

44. B – Sport
45. C – 7
46. D – A slide

Be Our Guest Restaurant

47. A - Lumiere
48. B – A bath
49. D – 50
50. C - 18

Enchanted Tales with Belle

51. B – Checkers
52. C – Blue
53. A – 18 years
54. D – 17

Gaston's

55. C – Gaston
56. B – 60

Under the Sea – Journey of the Little Mermaid

57. B – Ariel
58. C – Crabs
59. A – Accordion
60. D – 20

61. A – Helmet
62. C – 8
63. C – 6
64. B – Saxophone
65. A – Nasty
66. D – Cranes
67. D – Blue
68. C – Turtle
69. A – 3

Pinocchio Village Haus

70. C – Figaro
71. B – Green
72. D – Piece of cake
73. B – Soldier

Peter Pan's Flight

74. A – Crocodile
75. C - Mary
76. B – 3:55
77. A – December 27
78. D - Blue
79. D – Raggedy Anne
80. C – Deer
81. B - 7
82. A – "Help Me Mr. Smee!"
83. C – 12

It's a Small World

84. D – 13
85. C – 2
86. B – Sailed
87. B – 6

88. A – A windmill
89. A – Hearts
90. C – Owl
91. B – 6
92. D – Pink
93. C – 8
94. B – Sombreros
95. A – Guitar
96. C – Yellow
97. D – Fears
98. A – Aloha

Tangled

99. B – Finger sandwiches
100. D – He insisted
101. A – Rapunzel

Liberty Square

Liberty Square Riverboat

1. C - Tyranny
2. C – All Cargo
3. B – Horace Bixby
4. A – 100
5. D – Barefoot
6. A – Potters
7. B – Unfriendly spirits
8. C – Powhatan
9. A – Pirates

Hall of Presidents

10. D - Billboard
11. A – 1964

12. D – 8
13. C – Mount Vernon
14. A – Burden
15. C – Illinois
16. D – 11
17. A – Dedicate a cemetery
18. B – Big stick
19. A – October 28, 1929
20. A – Polio
21. D – 4
22. C – 35
23. B – The Battle Hymn of the Republic
24. B – Waste

The Haunted Mansion

25. C – Gun
26. D – Snake
27. A - Monocle
28. D – Taking a bath
29. C – Mourning
30. B – Corruptible
31. A – Danger
32. D – Bone
33. B – Ghost stories
34. A – Chills
35. C – Bell
36. C – 13
37. D – Axe
38. B – Silly
39. D – Guitar
40. B – 3
41. D – Ball and chain
42. A – MT Tomb
43. A – Repeal of the stamp act

The Great Walt Disney World Scavenger Hunt

Adventureland

1. D – 8

Swiss Family Robinson Treehouse

2. C – 1805
3. D – Swallow
4. A – Bible
5. C – Rum
6. D – Our small world
7. B – Ships log
8. B – Seashell

The Enchanted Tiki Room

9. A – Fredrick
10. B – In the audience
11. C – Hair
12. D – Juanita
13. A – Rosita
14. A – The shower
15. C – The gods
16. C – *Heigh Ho*

The Jungle Cruise

17. C – Quinine
18. C – Leech salt
19. D – Kittens
20. B – Daredevil trips over Schweitzer falls
21. B – Ivory
22. B – Chicken (really)
23. C – Skulls
24. D – Python
25. B – Green

26. C – 6
27. A – Hyena
28. B – Ginger
29. B – Albert Falls
30. A – Wiggling their ears
31. C – Skulls
32. D – Spears
33. C – They have their trunks on
34. C – Shrunken heads
35. A – Orangutan
36. B – Ganges
37. D – Run aground Sue
38. C – C.M. Cooken
39. A – Seymour Butz

Pirates of the Caribbean

40. B – Tell no tales
41. A – 4
42. A – The Wicked Wench
43. B – Carlos
44. A – Her flock
45. D – Rum
46. C – A grandfather clock
47. D – 3
48. B – A dog biscuit

Frontierland

Country Bear Jamboree

1. A – Bill
2. C – Fur coats
3. B – Beehive
4. C – Key of G
5. D – Shoot him

6. B – Raccoon
7. D – Richard Le Pere Jr.
8. A - $300.00

Frontierland Shooting Gallery

9. C – Heart
10. B – Frown
11. D – A saw
12. C – 35

Splash Mountain

13. A – 50 feet
14. C – Chesapeake
15. C - 9
16. B – Br'er Turtle
17. B – Br'er Frog
18. D – Critter Elixir
19. C – Muskrat
20. A – No fishing
21. D – Harmonica
22. B – Frog
23. C – Vultures
24. D – Pig
25. C – American flag

Briar Patch

26. A – Briar sweet briar
27. B – Whistler's Mother
28. D – 1:18
29. C – 8

Frontierland Railroad Station

30. B - $15,000.00
31. D – Armed stagecoach robbery
32. A – San Francisco
33. C – Red Cross Oak
34. B - Democracy

Big Thunder Mountain Railroad

35. A – 38
36. C – Clarkdale
37. A – Gum chewing
38. B – Tag
39. C – 2.38
40. D – James K. Polk
41. B – Weekly
42. A – Flash flood
43. C – 700 feet
44. B - Cow punching
45. B – Bunions
46. D - $5.00
47. C – Missing a work shift
48. A – Eat beans
49. D – Wilderness
50. C – 1867
51. B – Head lice

Tom Sawyer Island

52. B – Huck
53. D – The birds
54. C – Stop
55. A – Rifle Roost

Tomorrowland

Buzz Lightyear Space Ranger Spin

1. A – C
2. C – Sector 9
3. D – XP-37
4. C – Zurg Rules
5. B – Space Ace
6. A – Glendale
7. C – Stitch
8. B – Galaxy

Walt Disney's Carousel of Progress

9. C – 1964-65
10. D – Day
11. A – Valentine's day
12. B – Less than 7 days
13. C – 5 hours
14. D – St. Louis
15. D – The cat's meow
16. B – George Washington
17. A – Statue of Liberty
18. C – Yellow
19. B – Rat race
20. D – Boxing
21. C – Wallpapering
22. A – Root beer
23. B – Nutcrackers
24. C – 975

Monster's Inc. Laugh Floor

25. C – Racoon bar
26. B – Clean horns make healthy horns

27. A – Tuesday
28. B – The doors won't open

Tomorrowland Transit Authority PeopleMover

29. C – The sky
30. D – People watching
31. A – Planet
32. B – Watch your rollers
33. D – Astronauts
34. D – Mr. Johnson
35. C – 20th
36. A – Buzz Lightyear
37. B - Roz
38. B - 10

Epcot

Spaceship Earth

1. A – Judi Dench
2. B – 15 thousand years
3. C – Reeds
4. D – Phoenicians
5. B – Roads
6. A – Alexandria
7. B – Guttenberg
8. C – New York
9. D – California
10. C – 30,000

Mission Space

11. B – Plato
12. C – February 14, 1972
13. B – Impossible

The Great Walt Disney World Scavenger Hunt

14. B – Yuri Gagarin
15. A – February 7, 1984
16. D – Dalmatian
17. C – Sheldon Cooper
18. D - Training
19. D – Solid Hydrogen
20. B – 6,000
21. A – Astronaut
22. B – Mars
23. D – Activate hyper sleep
24. C – Meteor storm

The Land

25. B – Amy Larrick
26. D – Patchwork Quilt
27. A – Punishments

Living with the Land

28. C – Scythe
29. A - Alligator
30. D – Living
31. B – The tropics
32. D – Cactus
33. A – Bananas
34. C – One half
35. A – 27,000
36. B – Fishermen

Soarin' Around the World

37. A – Patrick Warburton
38. C – Mickey Ears
39. D – Little aviators
40. C – Matterhorn

41. B – Killer whale
42. B – Neuschwanstein Castle
43. D – Elephant
44. A – Kite flying
45. A – Mausoleum
46. D – Iguazu Falls
47. B – Paris
48. C – Epcot

The Seas with Nemo and Friends

49. C – Coral Caves
50. A – Pelican
51. D – Choppy
52. B – Mr. Ray
53. C – Fabio
54. C – Shell
55. B – Peach

SeaBase

56. A – Dolphin
57. D – Bright
58. A – 8 million
59. B – Calcium carbonate
60. C – Snapping its jaws
61. C – Mammals
62. A – Cartilage
63. D – Humpback whales

Journey Through Imagination with Figment

64. B – Shrink ray
65. D – Custodian
66. D – A suitcase
67. A – Chicken

68. C – Red
69. B – I O Z
70. C – Skunk
71. A – Tickle testing
72. D – Light bulb

World Showcase

Canada

1. A – 1790
2. C – Sunshine
3. C - 40 gallons

O' Canada

4. C – Martin Short
5. D – Horseshoe Falls
6. D – Fifty feet
7. B – Polar bears
8. A – Pro hockey player
9. A – The Rocky Mountains
10. C – 1912
11. D – Quebec
12. B – Tom Hanks
13. C – Soarin'

United Kingdom

14. A – Boxing day
15. B – Pig
16. A – 3
17. D – Skulls
18. D – Hatching

France

19. B – 103 feet

Morocco

20. A – 14th
21. C – Courtyard
22. D – 786
23. B – Souk
24. D – Kohl
25. C – Wedding
26. A – Fantasia

Japan

27. B – The sun goddess
28. C – Electricity

The American Adventure

29. B – Defending freedom
30. A – Globe
31. D – Children
32. C – Reaching for the stars
33. A – 1620
34. C – Fifty-nine
35. A – 1886
36. C – Harlem hell fighters

The American Adventure

37. D – Mark Twain
38. B – Pride
39. C – Pilgrims
40. A – King George III
41. C – The Declaration of Independence

The Great Walt Disney World Scavenger Hunt

42. D – Two changes
43. B – Their creator
44. C – Money
45. A – Lobster backs
46. B – *Uncle Tom's Cabin*
47. C – The Civil War
48. B – Philadelphia
49. C – Susan B. Anthony
50. A – Airplane
51. D – World War I
52. B – The Spirit of St. Louis
53. A – Franklin D. Roosevelt
54. C – Pearl Harbor attack
55. A – Tinker Bell
56. D – The Statue of Liberty

China

57. B – Gate of the Golden Sun
58. C – Terracotta Warriors

Reflections of China

59. A – Four-thousand miles
60. C – Poet
61. D – Tai Chi
62. B – Poem
63. D – Silk
64. A – Six months
65. A – Carve ice sculptures
66. B – Dragons
67. C – Twenty-four
68. D – The faces of its people

Norway

69. A – 13th
70. D – Vikings
71. D – Marathon runner
72. B – Troll

Frozen Ever After

73. C – 50%
74. A – Duke of Weselton
75. B – Summer Snow Day Celebration
76. D – Oaken
77. D – Sven
78. C – Three
79. A – Ice skating
80. B – Marshmallow
81. C – Rune stone

Mexico

82. A – Toltec
83. D – 1524
84. A – Calendar

Grand Fiesta Tour starring the Three Caballeros

85. C - Burrito
86. B – Volcano
87. D – Flying serape
88. D – Donald Duck
89. A – Where is Donald?
90. C – Red
91. D – Maracas

Disney Hollywood Studios
Hollywood Blvd
Oscar's Super Service

1. B – Bo
2. C – KLondike 5320
3. A – Ethyl
4. D – Muskegon, Michigan
5. B – Mohawk
6. D – $.19 9/10
7. C – JSW4B
8. C – 715
9. A – 5626
10. C – Anaheim
11. B - Born
12. B – Agent
13. D – *Autograph Hound*
14. A – Pluto's Toy Palace

Celebrity 5 & 10

15. C – Robert Reed
16. D – Pies
17. B – Jean Harlow

Adrian and Edith's

18. A – 13
19. D – Dragon
20. B – Twitterpated
21. D - Ostrich

The Brown Derby

22. D – 3377 Wilshire Blvd

23. B – Carol Channing
24. D – Jimmie Dodd
25. A – Mortimer Snerd
26. B – 2700

Sunset Blvd

1. C – American Tourister
2. D – Tower of Terror

Rockin' Roller Coaster Starring Aerosmith

3. A – Their manager
4. D – Black Les Paul
5. C – Do not play
6. D – Parking attendant
7. B – Street Emotion detail
8. A – A big tip
9. D – Civic center
10. C – Donuts

Twilight Zone Tower of Terror

11. A – 1928
12. B – October 31, 1939
13. C – Lower level
14. D – 908
15. C – *To Serve Man*
16. A – Pool
17. B – Dead
18. C – Engineering
19. D – A lightbulb
20. B - Auto insurance
21. A – Whiskey
22. B – Bananas
23. C – Quail eggs on toast points

The Great Walt Disney World Scavenger Hunt

Carthay Circle

24. C – Lillian Disney
25. A – 35 cents

Echo Lake

50's Prime Time Cafe

1. A – Matador and Bull
2. B – Art
3. C – Charles Dickens
4. D – Grapes
5. C – General Electric
6. A – *I Love Lucy*
7. D – Flour
8. B – April, 1952
9. A – Cookies
10. C – Gertie
11. B – California Crazy
12. C – T. Kirk
13. A – Actors
14. D - Baby Herman

Star Tours – The Adventure Continues

15. C – At At
16. A – Admiral Ackbar
17. B – Gate change
18. C – On approach
19. B – Cleared by customs
20. D – Bag pipes
21. A – *The Incredibles*
22. D – "Where's the snooze bar?"
23. B – To avoid paying duty fees
24. C – Buzz Lightyear

25. B – Selling defective lightsabers

Grand Avenue

1. C – Fozzie Bear
2. C – Spare change

Muppetvision 3-D

3. B – Sweetums
4. A – Link Hogthrob
5. C – Tippy top cookie guy
6. D – Sartorial accumulation division
7. C – My life as a mutt
8. B – Ten tiny tin toy boats
9. A – Stair trek
10. C – Spanky's Spectacular Spectacles
11. D – Neck Ruffs
12. B – Pig's in Space
13. A – Dog
14. A – An aquarium
15. D – Rizzo
16. C – Max
17. D – *Muppet Most Wanted*
18. B – Mickey Mouse
19. B – For the halibut
20. A – Chickens
21. C – Dusting
22. D – Banana cream pie
23. C – Sweetums
24. A – Swedish Chef

Stage 1 Store

25. D – Zero
26. C – Accountant

The Great Walt Disney World Scavenger Hunt

27. B – There's no such thing as net profits
28. C – Union jack
29. D – Linen
30. D – Murphy bed
31. C – Visitors
32. D – Flies
33. A – Cactus motel
34. B – Caperlite
35. C – Houdini
36. D – Ventilated

Mama Melrose Ristorante Italiano

37. C – Now you see it, now you don't
38. B – The Mona Lisa
39. A – America
40. C – Guy Lombardo
41. D – 51
42. B – A glass of wine
43. A – No kidding

PizzeRizzo

44. D – 8
45. C – Animal
46. B – Brooklyn
47. C – I'll treat you cheddar
48. A – Fish
49. D – 875
50. A – Rizzo

Toy Story Land

1. D – Woody
2. B – Yo yo
3. A – Blue

4. C - Jenga

Toy Story Mania

5. D - Rex
6. D – 122789 0216102
7. A – Bear
8. B – Rubber cement
9. C – Bo Peep
10. C – Uno
11. A – Mrs. Potato Head
12. B – Tomorrowland
13. D – One week
14. C – 2000 lbs.
15. C – 92
16. A – Simple Simon
17. A – Reading Railroad
18. B – Space Carnival
19. D – 12 million
20. D – Carnation pink
21. C – Dr. Malpractice
22. B – 50 Bzillion
23. C – Barney
24. A – *The Boy Scout Handbook*
25. A – Knick Knack
26. C – Pies
27. D – 18
28. B - $50.00
29. C – Stinky Pete's place
30. B – Slinky Dog
31. A – 62 pieces
32. D – Dominoes

The Great Walt Disney World Scavenger Hunt

Alien Swirling Saucers

33. C – Pizza
34. B – Gamma
35. A – Display courage
36. B – 13
37. D – Red
38. A – W
39. C – 3
40. B – Battle Creek

Andy's Lunchbox

41. D – Harmonica
42. C – Turtle
43. A – Juice box
44. C – Cheese
45. B – 102
46. D – 1913
47. A – Green
48. B – Cowboy hat
49. C – Ticonderoga

Slinky Dog Dash

50. B – Buster
51. C – James Industries
52. D – 425
53. D – Emeryville, Ca.
54. A – Toss Across
55. B – Wheezy
56. C – Camera
57. C - $19.95
58. D – Pick Up Snakes
59. A – Robert Goulet
60. D - *The Alpine Bounce*

Animation Courtyard

Walt, One Man's Dream

1. A – Marceline, Mo.
2. D – 1956
3. A – *Snow White and the Seven Dwarves*
4. C – Reciting the Gettysburg Address
5. B – Candy
6. B – *Alice's Spooky Adventure*
7. D – 1929
8. C – Carter's
9. A – Donald Duck
10. D – Shirley Temple
11. B – Figaro
12. C – *The Wise Little Hen*
13. D – Buddy Ebsen
14. A – Christmas day
15. C – *When you wish upon a star*
16. B – Tinker Bell
17. A – Dodie
18. B – 45 acres
19. A – Dumbo
20. B – New York
21. C – 1983
22. D – 325
23. C – Illness
24. A – Cardboard
25. B - $40.00
26. D – He created Mickey Mouse
27. D – Walt Disney
28. A – 1931
29. C – Carthay Circle Theater
30. B – *The Absent-Minded Professor*
31. D – *The Parent Trap*

32. C – Disneyland
33. A – *When you Wish Upon a Star*
34. B – Julie Andrews

The Voyage of the Little Mermaid

35. D – Monstro
36. B – Hemmingway
37. A – *The Old Man and the Sea*
38. C – Tinkerbell

Disney's Animal Kingdom

Discovery Island

1. C – Elephant

It's Tough to be a Bug

2. D – Pterodactyl
3. B - The Acorn Street Journal
4. A - Stink bug
5. B – Tarantula
6. C - *Hello Dung Lovers*
7. A - 26,000
8. C – Smell
9. C - One teaspoon
10. B – Picky
11. A – Black widow
12. D – 15
13. B – 40 feet
14. D – 5 million
15. D – Hi Mom
16. D – 800,000
17. B – Beetles
18. A - Jumping

19. B – 300 million years
20. C – Chili
21. D – Acorns
22. B – I'll be back
23. A – Churros
24. C – Pill bugs
25. B – Bug Doom
26. A – Rotten cupcake
27. D - Grasshoppers

Africa

1. C – Romantic
2. A – Animals
3. B – 1420
4. C – Poaching
5. D – Survey office

Kilimanjaro Safaris

6. B - Baobab tree
7. A – Tembo
8. C – Zebra
9. A – Crowned crane
10. C – Giraffe
11. D – 20 pounds
12. B – 20 hours
13. C – Hello
14. A – Giraffe
15. C – Ghosts
16. A – 6 minutes
17. B – Nile crocodile
18. D - Put them in their mouth
19. A - Helps digest their food
20. C – Ostrich

The Great Walt Disney World Scavenger Hunt

21. B - Protect the pride

Gorilla Falls Exploration Trail

22. C – ZU2298
23. D – Our children
24. A – Make excessive noise
25. B – The animals
26. D – Thistles
27. A – Jane Goodall
28. C – A nest
29. B – 5,000
30. A- Nile perch

Pandora – The World of Avatar

1. B – I see you
2. A – Do not run
3. D – Hunting

Avatar Flight of Passage

4. C – Sting bats
5. D – Select (hostile) ATMO
6. A – Reverse habitat destruction
7. B – James Cameron's birthday
8. B – 40,000 PSI
9. C – A ladder
10. D – 16:10
11. A – Injuries
12. D – Twenty minutes
13. B – Suppression agent
14. C – 2101
15. B – Keystone
16. A – Hellfire
17. C – Trees

18. D – Membrane
19. D – More activity
20. B – Samples
21. C – Embraced the flames
22. B – *IKRAN My Connection*
23. A – Earth equipment
24. C – Rock sample castings
25. D – Coffee mugs
26. A – Softball
27. B – Medical
28. C – Parasites
29. A – Common
30. D – Dr. Ogden

Asia

1. C – Bat cliffs
2. D – Lantern festival
3. A – Next season
4. D – Monday
5. B – Prayer
6. C – Mandarin

Maharaja Jungle Trek

7. A – 1544
8. B – Respectful
9. D – 7%
10. C – Deforestation
11. B – River water
12. C – Livestock
13. B – Rand

Expedition Everest – Legend of the Forbidden Mountain

14. A – Climbers
15. B – One Yeti foot
16. A – Ten
17. C – Dan Casteel
18. D – Stay centered
19. D – 37 Kilos
20. C – Electric underwear
21. B – The forbidden mountain
22. A – 75
23. C – 91530
24. A – Pema Djori
25. D – Tea
26. B – Crampons

Dinoland U.S.A

1. C – Exhumation
2. D – Pterodactyl
3. A – 52 feet
4. D – 1900

The Boneyard

5. C – 1947
6. B – Dr. Woo
7. B – T Rex
8. A – Diana Sore
9. C – His tail
10. D – Line dancing
11. C – 1968 van
12. B – Get to work!
13. A – Rejection
14. B – Rack of water pistols

15. D – 5

Primeval Whirl

16. C – Red
17. D – This really extincts
18. A - $ 2.00

Chester and Hester's Dinosaur Treasures

19. B – Existence
20. D – 3
21. C – Fossil foam
22. B – 1953
23. A – Pteranodon
24. C – Measuring sticks
25. A – Guard dino
26. D – LZS433
27. B - $.20 ½
28. A – 65 million
29. A – Sue

Dinosaur!

30. C – 1978
31. D – Western North America
32. B – Worldwide flooding
33. C – Bull dog like
34. B – Phylicia Rashad
35. A – In the past
36. D – Paleontologist
37. C – Cretaceous
38. B – Iguanodon
39. C – Flash photography
40. D – Vegetarian
41. A – Carnotaurus

Dino-bytes Snacks

42. D – King

Restaurantosaurus

43. B – 15244
44. C – One-way
45. A – Hawaiian shirt day
46. D – *Gertie the Dinosaur*
47. A – Animal
48. B – 11 pm
49. C – Bacchanal
50. D - Bisby, Az
51. B - Midas of the museum world
52. C - 55589-9054
53. A - 555-DINO
54. B - Handprints

www.ingramcontent.com/pod-product-compliance
Lightning Source LLC
Chambersburg PA
CBHW071152070526
44584CB00019B/2759